BATMAN™ & ROBIN™

THE MAKING OF THE MOVIE

MICHAEL SINGER

TITAN BOOKS

BATMAN & ROBIN
THE MAKING OF THE MOVIE
1 85286 836 8

Published by
Titan Books Ltd
42-44 Dolben St
London
SE1 0UP

First edition June 1997
10 9 8 7 6 5 4 3 2 1

British Library Cataloguing-in-Publication Data. A catalogue record for this book is available from the British Library.

Batman & Robin production photography by Christine Loss, Michael Garland, Jason Hubbard, and Robert Isenberg.
Visual effects images supplied by BUF Compagnie and Warner Digital.
Comic covers used by kind permission of DC Comics.

ACKNOWLEDGEMENTS

My gratitude is extended to every single member of the cast and crew who so generously offered their time and knowledge, even in the midst of the filmmaking hurricane called *Batman & Robin*; of course, to all of my friends and colleagues at DC Comics and Warner Bros., who helped to spirit me through the process, and to all at Titan Books, especially Katy Wild, Chris Teather, Bob Kelly and Adam Newell, for bringing the project to the shelves. This book is dedicated to them, and especially to my always patient, ever-loving shrine maidens: my wife, Yuko; daughter, Miyako; and brand-new baby, Kimiko, whose arrival during production happily doubled my efforts both professionally and personally - *Michael Singer.*

ABOUT THE AUTHOR

Michael Singer is a motion picture unit publicist and author who has written *Batman Forever: The Official Movie Book, Batman Returns: The Official Movie Book* and *The Making of Oliver Stone's Heaven and Earth*. He is also the editor and author of the annually published standard reference book *Michael Singer's Film Directors: A Complete Guide*, now in its twelfth edition. In addition to the last three *Batman* films, Singer has also served as unit publicist on such films as *Sphere, Jerry Maguire, A Time to Kill, Nixon, Natural Born Killers, Heaven and Earth, Free Willy*, and *Grumpy Old Men*.
He is based in San Francisco, where he lives with his wife and daughters.

The Publishers would also like to thank Michael Singer; everyone at DC Comics particularly Dawn Evans, Phyllis Hume,Trent Duffy, Larry Daley, Elisabeth Vincentelli, Dana Brass and Rob Simpson, for their tireless help with this project; and everyone at Warner Bros. Consumer Products, especially Jess Garcia, Pallie Jones, Hank Kanalz, Julie Ruttenberg, Shannon Ryan, Regan Schaar, Susan Stern, LaDonna Williams, and Mary Yedlin, for smoothing the book's progress.

Printed in Wales by Stephens & George, Merthyr Industrial Estate, Dowlais, Merthyr Tydfil.

CONTENTS

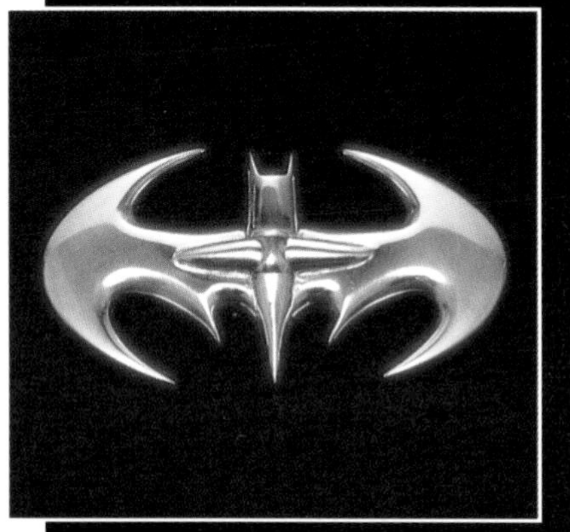

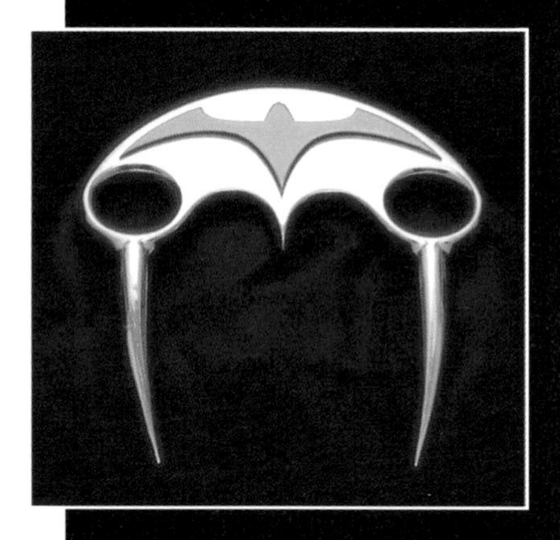

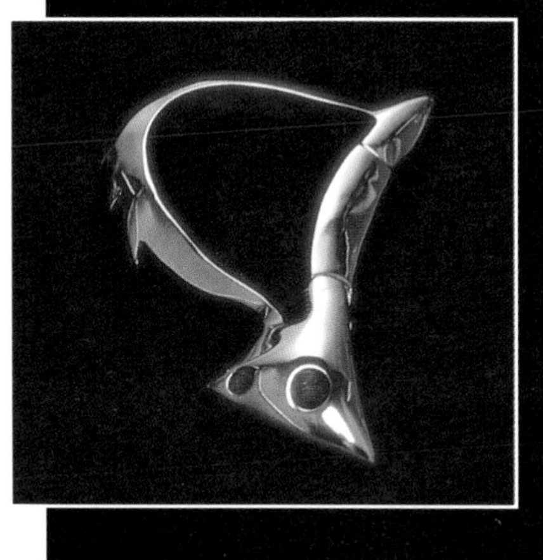

MEET THY CREATOR

What would it have been like on such recent films as *Hamlet, Sense and Sensibility* or *Anna Karenina* had William Shakespeare, Jane Austen or Leo Tolstoy spent time on the sets? The cast and crew would have been suitably awestruck, overwhelmed and perhaps even a little bit intimidated by the presence of such giants.

Thus, each time *Batman* creator Bob Kane strode onto the Warner Bros. sets of *Batman & Robin*, many reacted in similar fashion. Without Kane's blast of inspiration nearly 60 years ago, nothing on the soundstage—sets, actors, crew or their paychecks—could possibly have existed.

So *this* is what it's like to meet your maker. Many of *Batman & Robin*'s personnel grew up on *Batman* comics, watched the TV show, lived the dreams of Gotham City and were now working their hearts out to make the legend a "reality" once again. No wonder Kane elicited such universal respect and appreciation during his numerous set visits.

Once Kane seated himself on the soundstage, a line immediately formed to pay homage to this charter member of comic-book royalty. The Great Man often drew a black-ink portrait of the Caped Crusader for these admirers, his trademark signature adorning a corner of the sheet.

It was clear that Kane relished the attention, even as he registered astonishment at how his creation just grows and grows on screen. "These sets are super spectacular, they're like something out of Cecil B. De Mille," enthuses Kane on a cool day in October, leaving the rooftop Botanical Garden set for some fresh air. "The sets in the other *Batman* movies were also great, but this is really something special."

Kane had good reason to spend so much time on the Botanical Garden set, for prominently featured in the spectacular charity ball sequence as Gossip Gerty—Gotham's favorite busybody—was his wife, actress Elizabeth Sanders. Kane glows with pride as he discusses Sanders's contribution in a role that she first created in *Batman Forever*. "Gossip Gerty is a fun throwback to

This page: *Artist Bob Kane re-creates the historic moment when he invented Batman in a classic frame from the DC Comics vaults* **(below)**; *Kane in costume for a cameo appearance in the Botanical Garden Charity Ball sequence* **(bottom)**.

Opposite: *The latest incarnation of Bob Kane's creation—George Clooney as Batman* **(top)**; *Kane with Elizabeth Sanders, who has portrayed Gossip Gerty in* Batman Forever *and* Batman & Robin **(bottom)**. *She is also Mrs. Bob Kane.*

powerful 1940s gossip columnists like Louella Parsons and Hedda Hopper," Kane notes, "and Elizabeth is adorable. She has presence that just pops out on the screen."

Kane also reacts exuberantly when asked about the cast assembled for *Batman & Robin*. "I feel George is the best Batman of all. He's suave, elegant, has a great profile with a strong chin, like the features of Batman in the comic books. Arnold Schwarzenegger's Mr. Freeze is just incredible, and Uma Thurman is superlative as Poison Ivy, every man's desire with her flaming red hair and beautiful costumes. Chris O'Donnell is back, and he's a tremendous Robin. He's a great personality, and he really delivers the goods. And Alicia Silverstone is such a cute Batgirl...teenagers will love her!"

The film's grandiose sets are "in keeping with the spirit of the original comic books," Kane believes. "When I started writing the

character with the late Bill Finger—the unsung hero of *Batman*—he would bring giant settings and props into the story, and then build the plot around them. We would have a giant telescope or laboratory, like the ones in this movie, or stage a fight on top of the Statue of Liberty."

Kane is delighted with the turn his creation has taken under the direction of Joel Schumacher. As an official consultant to *Batman & Robin*, Kane proposes his opinions and ideas regarding the script and other matters to Schumacher and screenwriter Akiva Goldsman. On set, Kane positions himself right next to the director in front of the bank of video assist monitors on which they view the shots as they're being filmed, offering advice and bantering with Schumacher in an *Odd Couple* way.

"Joel has great vision," Kane says with enthusiasm, "and he's an ardent comic-book fan from way back. Joel was kind enough to write the preface for the revised edition of my book *Batman and Me*, and there's a wonderful phrase he had that sticks in my mind: 'The reveries of children sometimes become the vocation of adults.' Batman was Joel's favorite comic-book character when he was a boy, and I'm thrilled that he's the one who's inherited the *Batman* movies."

And then Bob Kane pauses to chat with yet another swarm of fans and well-wishers from the *Batman & Robin* crew, unabashedly loving it all.

"ONE MORE ONE . . ."

Within sight of the *Queen Mary* in Long Beach Harbor is a huge white geodesic dome, its 140,000-square-foot interior originally constructed to display the hulking Spruce Goose aircraft, Howard Hughes's magnificent folly. These days, the Long Beach Seaport Dome has a very different function: it's tantamount to the world's largest movie soundstage.

On September 11, 1996, the Seaport Dome is a noisy construction site, light streaming down through a large irislike opening in the roof. The very next morning it is transformed into a hushed cathedral of filmmaking—the Church of the Caped Crusader—as the disembodied, almost spooky voice of first assistant director/co-producer Bill Elvin, announcing "Quiet please for camera," reverberates through the gigantic building.

All is silent, save for the quiet hum of the Panavision camera and the dialogue delivered by Alicia Silverstone and Michael Gough in the first scene scheduled for filming. The walls of the Seaport Dome melt away, replaced by the stately environs of Wayne Manor. The illusion of a fantasy world layered atop the real one is nearly complete, and the first of *Batman & Robin*'s nearly 100 days of principal photography is underway.

Opposite, bottom right: *The gigantic Gotham Museum set under construction on Warner Bros. Stage 16.*
This page: *Batman comic-book covers through the ages, and the man who started it all, the legendary Bob Kane.*

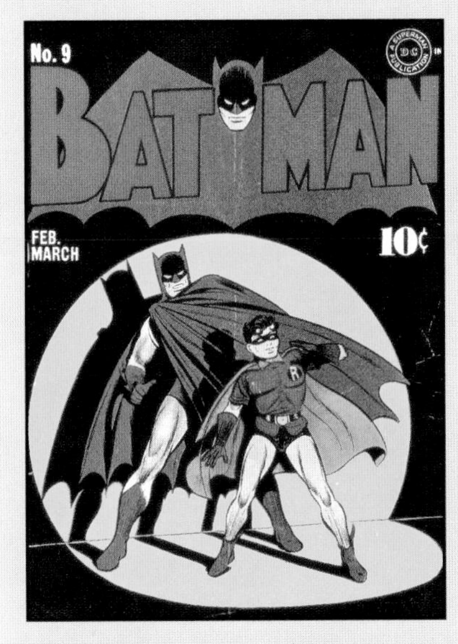

It begins, of course, with two hungry, ambitious teenage cartoonists, Bob Kane and Bill Finger. Laboring on two-page comedy material for DC Comics in the late 1930s, Kane ultimately turns to more serious fare with such stories as *Spark Stevens, Rusty and His Pals* and *Clip Carson*.

Then he has an epiphany. Inspired in part by Leonardo da Vinci's notebook drawing of a flying contraption called an Ornithopter—a kind of sled with bat-wings—Kane, in collaboration with Finger, contrives a new hero called *The Bat-Man*. Making its debut in a May 1939 issue of *Detective Comics*, *The Bat-Man* is an immediate sensation with readers and propels the character on an odyssey through what has now been six decades of development, alteration and interpretation in comics, movie serials, a 1960s TV series,

Below: *The fine art of body casting;*
Below right: *Senior set designer James Bayliss.*

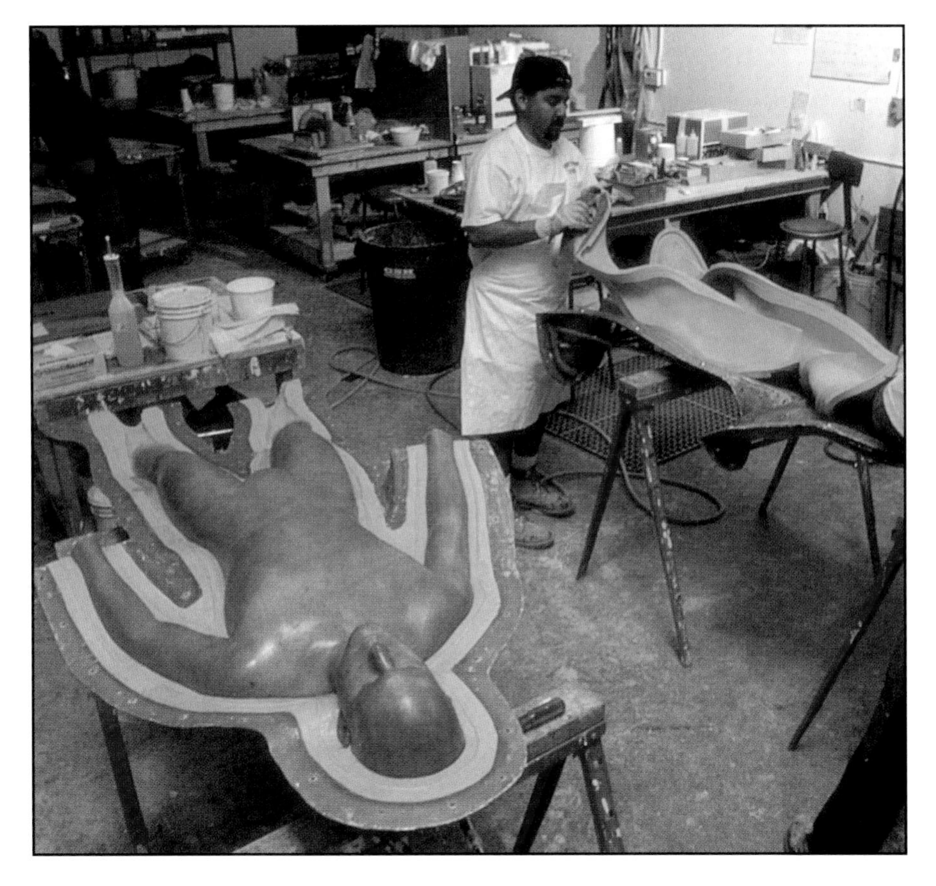

graphic novels and, finally, the 1989 film *Batman*, directed by Tim Burton. That film is an instant phenomenon, and results in a tremendously successful 1992 follow-up, *Batman Returns*, with Burton directing again.

Cut to 1994. The talented director Joel Schumacher is on location in Memphis, Tennessee, for Warner Bros.' film of John Grisham's best-seller *The Client*. A phone call from Bob Daly and Terry Semel, the chairmen of the studio, announces that a company jet will spirit Schumacher back to Burbank for an important meeting.

"I thought, Uh-oh. This is it. They're firing me," the filmmaker recalls.

But that was the last thing on Daly and Semel's minds. In fact, the imperial summons was to offer Schumacher "Warner Bros.' most important franchise."

Schumacher admits in retrospect that he was terrified by the invitation to reinvent Batman on film. Those who worked on *Batman Forever* remember how often Schumacher turned his jokes on himself in a self-deprecating manner. "I hope all of you have your next jobs," the director would say while watching the dailies of a particularly outrageous sequence, "because if they let me direct again after this, it's a miracle!"

Instead, *Batman Forever* was a wonder in itself, with the character receiving a vibrant, sexy new infusion by Schumacher and his tremendous support team. The film set a new record for the biggest opening weekend in the history of movies.

"I really didn't know that *Batman Forever* was going to be as successful as it turned out," Schumacher notes. "I think sometimes it's easier to analyze failure, because you can look at the mistakes you made. But the kind of success at the box office and with audiences that we had with *Batman Forever* is like catching lightning in a bottle.

"It's an interesting phenomenon when you make movies because by the time the

Right: *Director Joel Schumacher.*
Below: *Poison Ivy (Uma Thurman) is attended to by her faithful and deadly lackey, Bane (Jeep Swenson).*

film opens in theatres our experiences are finished and you're basically helpless to do anything more about the situation. I was traveling from Hong Kong to Australia when I got the phone call from the studio telling me that we broke all the records with *Batman Forever*, and as thrilled as I was, I had already given the movie away—to the audience."

THE MAN WHO LOVES MOVIES

"We don't make movies for ourselves," Joel Schumacher often says, which is only partially true. The pure joy that the filmmaker takes in the process is infectious. It trickles down to the rest of the cast and crew, making Schumacher's sets a terrifically entertaining place to be. Casually adorned in his own very particular style, the tall, elegantly proportioned Schumacher cuts a dashing, youthful figure. Welcoming to all on-set guests—especially children—Schumacher is nonetheless utterly fixed on the job at hand.

Those who have worked with the director become familiar with some of his signature verbal motifs: "One more one," indicating the need for another take of a particular shot; "This one's for the actors," giving his cast the opportunity of doing whatever makes them happy for one last take, even after Schumacher is already satisfied with what's been shot; "That was *fabulous*!," Schumacher's favorite superlative, and one that he uses whenever he's delighted at how well his cast has performed. One Schumacher phrase that nobody wants to hear is a tersely delivered "Do not mistake my kindness for weakness," an occasional reminder that his affability and friendliness are not synonyms for tolerance of bungles, screw-ups or unnecessary chatting.

Schumacher's lack of pretension is one trait he shares with great studio directors

Below right: *Director Joel Schumacher with Elizabeth Sanders (Gossip Gerty).*

of the past. Like them, Schumacher takes great pride rather than umbrage in being considered a "commercial" director. "Is 'commercial' a dirty word?" Schumacher inquires. "Is it a crime to make movies that audiences actually *want* to see?"

In fact, Schumacher sits comfortably between art and commerce. "It's a tightrope," he declares, "because if you swing too far to art for its own sake it becomes self-serving and pompous, and if you're too much on the side of commerce, why get up in the morning? I try and choose projects which both excite me and are, hopefully, appealing to a wide audience."

Schumacher is a highly versatile filmmaker who has proved himself equally adept at youth-oriented drama (*St. Elmo's Fire*), horror-comedy (*The Lost Boys*), romantic comedy-drama (*Cousins*), science fantasy (*Flatliners*), gritty social realism (*Falling Down*), compelling courtroom drama (*The Client* and *A Time to Kill*) and, of course, the extraordinarily inventive *Batman Forever*.

Before *Batman & Robin*, Schumacher's two most recent films–*Batman Forever* and *A Time to Kill*–both grossed in excess of $100 million at U.S. box offices, and these smash hits, added on his previous successes, garnered him the National Association of Theatre Owners' 1997 Director of the Year at their ShoWest Convention.

It's a long way to come for the working-class kid from Queens, New York, who grew up fatherless, dreaming of making enough of a living to make things more comfortable for his mother, who passed away just as he was at the cusp of fulfilling his dreams. Schumacher studied design and display at the Parsons School of Design and began his career in the entertainment industry as an art director for TV commercials before becoming costume designer for such films as Woody Allen's *Sleeper* and *Interiors*, Herbert Ross's *The Last of Sheila* and Paul Mazursky's *Blume in Love*.

Below left: *Production designer Barbara Ling's work also encompassed costumes, vehicles, and gadgetry.*

Schumacher then wrote the screenplays for the Motown-sound-infused musical *Sparkle* and the funk-driven hit comedy *Car Wash*. He made his directing debut with the telefilm *The Virginia Hill Story*, followed by his award-winning television movie *Amateur Night at the Dixie Bar and Grill*. *The Incredible Shrinking Woman* marked his feature-film directing debut, followed by *D.C. Cab*, for which he also wrote the screenplay.

Then came *St. Elmo's Fire*, based on a screenplay that Schumacher wrote with Carl Kurlander, which crystallized an entire social era and established, among other things, the director's radar-sharp casting ability.

It wasn't long after *Batman Forever* stormed into theatres that Warner Bros. asked Schumacher if he would be interested in taking on the next chapter of the series. Schumacher was still recuperating from *Forever*'s massive success. "I was finding my way on that film," he says, "and so did most of my colleagues, because it was the first *Batman* film we had worked on. I don't think any of us expected or even dreamed that *Batman Forever* would be so accepted.

"So when Bob Daly and Terry Semel asked me to direct another *Batman* film, I called Barbara Ling, our great production designer, and asked if she wanted to do another one. She said, 'Joel...we haven't even *scratched* the surface!' I think I had that feeling too, because I felt that what we were able to bring to *Batman Forever* was a lot of humor, color and action, and if audiences liked that, we could bring them even more fun and games."

ENTER THE SCRIBE

Those "fun and games" would be devised by Schumacher and screenwriter Akiva Goldsman, who had already collaborated with the director on *The Client*, *Batman Forever* and *A Time to Kill*. This New York native cleverly infused *Batman Forever* with equal dollops of human drama and humor, simultaneously respecting and innovating the legend. The son of two prominent child psychologists, Goldsman was the perfect man to layer the extravagant action of *Batman & Robin* over the sometimes painful emotional traumas that are at the heart of the matter of Gotham City's Dark Knight.

Right: *A caring Barbara Wilson (Alicia Silverstone) attends to her desperately ill uncle, (Michael Gough).* **Middle, left:** *Mr. Freeze (Arnold Schwarzenegger) in the secret chamber that protects his cryogenically frozen wife, Nora (Vendela Thommessen).* **Middle, right:** *Screenwriter Akiva Goldsman.* **Bottom:** *In a flashback, Bruce Wayne (Eric Lloyd) and a younger Alfred (Jon Simmons) place flowers on the grave of the boy's murdered parents.*

Goldsman was returning with Schumacher from a location scout for *A Time to Kill* when the subject of another *Batman* film first came up. "The advance press screening results had just come in for *Batman Forever*. They were very positive, and industry people were excited. Joel got this kind of elfin gleam in his eye and said, 'I think they're going to ask us for another one.' I was very flattered to be part of 'us' at that moment. Then Joel started throwing out some ideas, and I started throwing back some ideas, and by the end of the plane trip we had the skeleton of our story."

Goldsman worked side by side with Schumacher in 1995 during filming of *A Time to Kill* on its Mississippi locations, and then returned home to write the *Batman & Robin* script. The transition between projects was difficult but fun. "In a reality-based picture like *A Time to Kill*," explains Goldsman, "you can end a scene on a poignant look, or someone walking through a door and closing it behind them. On a *Batman* movie, there'd better be the flapping of a cape as somebody leaps out a window, or a giant building exploding before the sequence is over. It's really fun to switch gears, although sometimes there's grinding as you hit the clutch!"

Schumacher and Goldsman challenged themselves to develop a terrifically entertaining new adventure for Batman and Robin, while again including enough human drama to engage mature adults as much as their more viscerally oriented children. The resulting story is, beneath the exciting and humorous surface, about the degree to which some will go to eliminate loss and grief from their lives. "Essentially, *Batman* is about how we as individuals reckon with loss," confirms Goldsman. "I assume that was Bob Kane's conscious or unconscious intention when he developed the character's origins. And so, I think for the *Batman* stories to be rooted in any kind of emotional authenticity, they have to start there. It becomes rather difficult to tell the same sad story over and over, especially with *Batman* movies.

"So in *Batman & Robin* we play less

Left: *The cover of this* Batman *comic book from the DC vaults accurately predicts an important* Batman & Robin *subplot.*

Bottom left: *Another vintage comic introduced readers to Mr. Zero, who would be redubbed Mr. Freeze for the ABC television series, and beyond.*

Below: *The deadly duo of Poison Ivy (Uma Thurman) and Mr. Freeze (Arnold Schwarzenegger).*

Opposite: *Batgirl's comic-book introduction, and her reincarnation in* Batman & Robin, *thanks to Alicia Silverstone.*

with how wounded Batman is over this past tragedy and more with the potential loss of what he loves now. The primary trauma is Bruce's potential loss of Alfred, this surrogate parent whom he loves as much as anyone on the planet."

Every *Batman* movie needs a great arch-villain or two, and for *Batman & Robin*, Schumacher and Goldsman chose the ever-fascinating and deadly combo of Mr. Freeze and Poison Ivy.

Mr. Freeze made his first appearance in *Batman* #121 (February 1959) as Mr. Zero, a scientist whose exposure to a freezing chemical solution forced him to live in a

subzero suit. His name was changed to Mr. Freeze for the ABC-TV series *Batman* in 1966, and the popular character was portrayed by three actors during the program's run—most memorably, Otto Preminger, whose Teutonic, bald-pated menace presaged Arnold Schwarzenegger's even richer interpretation in *Batman & Robin*.

Poison Ivy, a.k.a. Dr. Pamela Isley, made her own smashing debut in *Batman* #181 (June 1966), a botanist gone bad who can kill with a kiss. Her other weapon is her sheer sexuality. Poison Ivy has never been portrayed before by a live actor, although she's a popular villainess on the *Batman & Robin* animated series.

In developing the script, Goldsman and Schumacher interwove the fates of these previously unrelated characters. "Both Mr. Freeze and Poison Ivy share something, which is a kind of noble initiative," notes Goldsman. "They are characters who are, in a weird way, potentially heroic, in that they were both trying to save the world. Mr. Freeze was a great scientist who had been working on life-preserving technologies even before his wife fell ill, and Pamela Isley wants to give plants a fighting chance in a world of ravaged forests and killing pollution. As such, this gives these villains much more drive and nobility. They have a further distance to travel to become evil, and a potential to return to good, Mr. Freeze in particular. He, like our heroes, is reckoning with loss."

For *Batman & Robin*, Schumacher and Goldsman have also resurrected Batgirl for a new generation. The first Batgirl was Betty Kane, niece of Batwoman, in the 1950s, but it was Barbara Gordon—daughter of Gotham Police Commissioner James Gordon—who is more generally known to fans. She made her first appearance in *Detective Comics* #359 (January 1967). William Dozier, executive producer of the *Batman* TV series, obtained a copy of the new comic and immediately introduced the character in the series (she was played by Yvonne Craig).

This jump-started Batgirl's popularity, and she's been a familiar presence ever since in both the comics and the animated series. However, she's been revised for the new film. "We re-conceptualized Batgirl for a few reasons," Goldsman explains. "When you have a lot of characters, you need to create relationships so that they can be brought together. We tied Barbara to Alfred as his niece rather than retain her as Commissioner Gordon's daughter, because Alfred is a more central character in our story. And by re-creating her as an orphan, we echo both Bruce and Dick's plight."

Joel Schumacher adds that "I didn't realize that there were so many young girls who were *Batman* fans, and as I looked around I noticed that there weren't any teenage super heroines in our culture. Fortunately, Batgirl did exist."

Both Goldsman and Schumacher returned to the wellspring of DC Comics for inspiration as they worked on the script. Schumacher explains, "The comic books have had so many extraordinary artists since Bob Kane started it all in 1939. Whenever I start to prepare a *Batman* movie, I always go right to the source. I just get piles and piles of *Batman* comic books, and really get inspired."

COMPANY... ATTENTION!

If Joel Schumacher is *Batman & Robin's* undisputed commander in chief, then Peter Macgregor-Scott can certainly qualify as its general. The military allusions are intentional. The huge logistics of the film were tantamount to a large-scale military operation, and Macgregor-Scott, who also produced *Batman Forever*, is attuned to every minuscule detail of the campaign.

Recalling the genesis of *Batman & Robin* in his mobile production trailer wedged between Stages 21 and 22 on the Warner lot—from the relatively comfortable vantage point of three quarters through the film's shooting—Macgregor-Scott can't help but laugh at the memory of when he was invited back into the Batcave.

"The first reaction is 'Oh, God.' The second reaction is 'Thank you, God.' And the third reaction is 'God Almighty!'

"The challenge and the fun of it," the producer continues, "is to make it fresh. Technically, we're more advanced now than we were two years ago. There are more available tools for the process, including CGI [computer-generated images] and other visual effects technologies."

His vocation has always been to accomplish the impossible. He's the man studios get when they need to mount a spectacular smash-up between a full-size train and a bus (*The Fugitive*) or to secure a working battleship to serve as a movie location for several months (*Under Siege*).

On *Batman & Robin*, nothing—but nothing—has escaped Macgregor-Scott's vision. "I'm very hands-on, and I know every shot that's being done by the main, second and visual effects units. *Batman Forever* was seamless, but I think *Batman & Robin* will be even more so, which is amazing considering that there will be something like 3000 specific, different pieces of action on film."

Macgregor-Scott and Schumacher have one of contemporary film's great produc-

Previous page, bottom: *Producer Peter Macgregor-Scott* **(right)** *in a downtown Los Angeles location with associate producer Mitchell Dauterive.*

This page, bottom: *New York-based executive producers Benjamin Melniker* **(left)** *and Michael E. Uslan visit the Long Beach Seaport Dome location.*

er/director relationships, which the former attributes to each man's ability to simply understand what the other requires. "Joel's strength is with the actors and the creative vision of the movie. My strength is in getting it all ready for him," Macgregor-Scott says with simple directness.

The pair amassed one of the largest, most talented creative and support teams in Hollywood memory, with about 60 percent of the *Batman Forever* crew returning for another swing through the world of the Caped Crusader. Among the key personnel:

That deep, authoritative voice continually heard on the set belonged to first assistant director William M. Elvin, a *Batman Forever* veteran who for this film also graduates to the position of co-producer, a tribute to his organizational skills and importance to the production.

Associate producer Mitchell Dauterive served in the same capacity on *Batman Forever*. On the last day of principal photography, Dauterive had bittersweet feelings: "It's been a lot of hard work and a lot of struggles along the way. Now that we've crossed most of the hurdles, it just seems like it's been a lot of fun."

Working for the fourth time as executive producers, after *Batman*, *Batman Returns* and *Batman Forever*, are the New York City-based team of Benjamin Melniker and Michael E. Uslan, who had the foresight and wisdom to obtain the motion picture rights to *Batman* in 1980 and the faith and tenacity to wait almost a decade before it became an on-screen reality.

Unit production manager Barry Waldman began work in March 1996. "I remember thinking that we had six months until shooting started in September, which was more than enough time for prep. But in fact, we could have used *another* six months. There's nothing small about *Batman & Robin*. This movie is a monster that has to be fed."

The huge, highly talented support staff included production associate Diane Sabatini, assistant production associates John Kreidman and Robin Mulcahy, and the adjutants to the two kingpins: Joel Schumacher's aides Bettina Rose and Eli Richbourg, and Macgregor-Scott's Lisa Reardon. Not to mention the department without which no one could ever survive: accounting, under production controller Jackie Baugh.

Cinematographer Stephen Goldblatt takes a light reading before cameras roll on the battle royale between Batman (George Clooney) and Mr. Freeze (Arnold Schwarzenegger) in the Gotham Observatory, with projected planets swirling behind them.

CINEMATOGRAPHER STEPHEN GOLDBLATT: HE'S GOT THE LOOK!

Shimmering, stunning and atmospheric, the push-the-envelope cinematography of *Batman & Robin* is the domain of Stephen Goldblatt, whose work on *Batman Forever* brought him an Oscar nomination. A carefully modulated symphony of color and light, the design of *Batman & Robin*'s look was achieved through much experimentation and painstaking toil.

"Both of these *Batman* films have been fun in retrospect," says Goldblatt. "I'm enormously proud of the results and I never would have missed the experience. But they also scared me to death."

Goldblatt had definite ideas in mind

when he began his work on *Batman & Robin*. "*Batman Forever* was a living comic book, and this one is even more so, more fantastical. Joel wanted the story to be amplified into comic operatic mythology."

Just one example of Goldblatt's trailblazing was his idea for visually enhancing the climactic showdown between Batman and Mr. Freeze in the Gotham Observatory. "I had an idea of placing this final battle against projections of whirling planets and starscapes," says Goldblatt. "We found specialized projectors in Paris and had 40 of them shipped to Los Angeles for this purpose." It took the director of photography four months to adapt them for film use, but it finally worked, to extraordinary effect.

Goldblatt's revolutionary approach to *Batman & Robin* demanded that he call upon the services of such specialists as aerial camera rigging maestro Earl Wiggins and special lighting supervisor John Tedesco. For the massive Gotham Museum set, Wiggins created a flying rig that can travel 200 feet through the set while rising up from the floor to the ceiling. Tedesco was charged by Goldblatt to "bring in the most state-of-the-art theatrical type of computerized lighting equipment that exists, which has really put us on the cutting edge of film lighting."

"Stephen's a visionary," states Tedesco. "He was very demanding on *Batman Forever*, always looking and craving new technology and color and excitement. This movie is tenfold what it was on the last one."

Bottom: *Stephen Goldblatt, aloft in the Observatory with a Panavision camera.*

FIRST-RATE SECOND UNIT

Doing what comes naturally on the Gotham Museum set, Peter Macdonald has just finished staging and filming stunts that defy logic, pyrotechnics that dazzle the eye and other pieces of rip-roaring action that will add immeasurably to the film's already heightened adrenaline level.

Blessed with a dry British wit that also helps keep him sane, Macdonald heeded the call and galloped across the "pond" from Britain when Joel Schumacher and Peter Macgregor-Scott invited him to direct *Batman & Robin*'s second unit. This was no small task: the second unit had its own 80-day shooting schedule, including some of the film's more challenging action beats and stunts. But with Macdonald at the helm, Schumacher and Macgregor-Scott could be at ease that all would be handled brilliantly, for their second unit director handled such chores on the first *Batman*

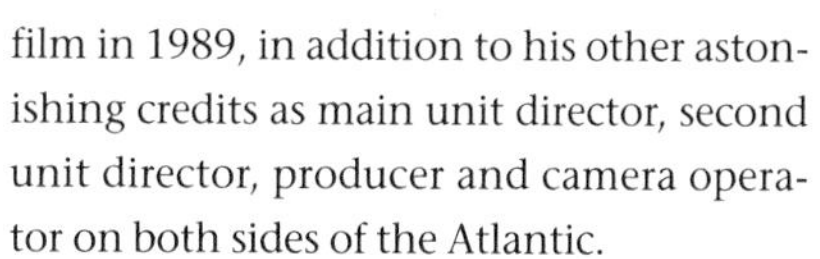

film in 1989, in addition to his other astonishing credits as main unit director, second unit director, producer and camera operator on both sides of the Atlantic.

For *Batman & Robin*, the two British "MacPeters"—as Macgregor-Scott and Macdonald came to be known—assembled a powerhouse second unit crew. Among the talented bunch were production supervisor Jacqueline George; director of photography Jamie Anderson; a team of hardworking assistant directors, including John Radulovic, J. J. Linsalata, Maura McKeown and Michael Risoli; Macdonald's enthusiastic assistant, Heidi Leigh; costume supervisor Marjorie Chan; property master Tim Wiles; and second unit stunt coordinator Steve Davison.

"Lots of people outside of the film busi-

Opposite page, bottom: *Co-producer/first assistant director William M. Elvin* **(left)** *on location with producer Peter Macgregor-Scott.*

ness don't really know what a second unit director actually does," admits the soft-spoken Macdonald, "and that's absolutely fine. Because when you get it right, no one should know who has shot what. You have to make sure that your work fits in neatly, without a seam, into the first unit's work. This is easy when you're working on a *Batman* film, because they're so well thought out."

Macdonald and Schumacher worked closely to ensure that the Briton was fulfilling the first unit's needs and vision. "Joel is extremely supportive and has no ego about my contributions to the film. We go through storyboards together, he makes sure that it's his vision that's going up on the screen, which is very important. After a while, I come to automatically understand what his vision is.

"*Batman & Robin* is so interesting because there's technology that's probably being used for the first time in almost every respect," Macdonald notes. "Barbara Ling's sets are just unbelievable, and Stephen Goldblatt, the cinematographer, is approaching lighting in a very different way. Everyone is learning new ways of doing things, and for me, it's an eye-opener. I mean, having just directed a film in England on a four-week shoot, coming to this was quite a sensation, you know?"

STARS OVER GOTHAM

"I did not expect to get such a great cast," states Joel Schumacher unequivocally. "You know, that's very rare in the fourth of a film series. Things sometimes begin to wind down at this point, and I think having such an exciting group of actors stimulated us all."

The first task at hand was to fill the Batsuit, since Val Kilmer, *Batman Forever*'s star, chose to journey on to other projects. Schumacher's casting instinct led him directly to George Clooney, who has in recent years rocketed into stardom on television's *ER*. Recalls Schumacher: "I saw George in *From Dusk Till Dawn* and recognized immediately that he not only had looks and talent, but real charisma. When I actually drew Batman's cowl onto George's face in a newspaper ad for the film, he looked perfect.

"Michael Keaton and Val Kilmer were both wonderful as Batman," Schumacher continues, "but I think George is the best of all. He's very much a man, a wonderful actor and of course, extremely handsome. He looks very much like Bruce Wayne in the comic books. George has also brought a real humanity and humor to the piece, an accessibility that I don't think anybody else has been able to.

"George is also dynamic with Chris O'Donnell, who has matured since the last film. Chris has really grown into his looks and as a performer. Since *Batman Forever*, Chris has carried movies on his own, which is a great responsibility. So when you see George and Chris together on-screen as Bruce Wayne and Dick Grayson, you totally believe that they would be friends."

Schumacher took great pleasure in casting his arch-villains. "Among the things that keep Batman so fresh, in comic books, TV and now film, are the marvelous villains.

"I was always crazy about Mr. Freeze from television, and Arnold Schwarzenegger was my only choice. He's a great action star, of course, but he has a great sense of humor, which is crucial to the *Batman* movies."

For Poison Ivy, Uma Thurman was Schumacher's one and only choice. "I've always wanted to work with Uma Thurman. The first time I saw her in a film was in *The Adventures of Baron Munchausen* as Venus. When that shell opened revealing her in imitation of Botticelli's painting, I said, '*Who* is that gorgeous girl?' I think to find someone that beautiful who's also such a wonderful actress is very rare."

How about the newest addition to the forces of good, Batgirl? "Alicia Silverstone is an extraordinary young woman, and of course, beautiful and talented. She's very popular with young audiences, and I thought it would be nice to give them a young heroine who was as intelligent, strong-willed and dedicated to justice as the men."

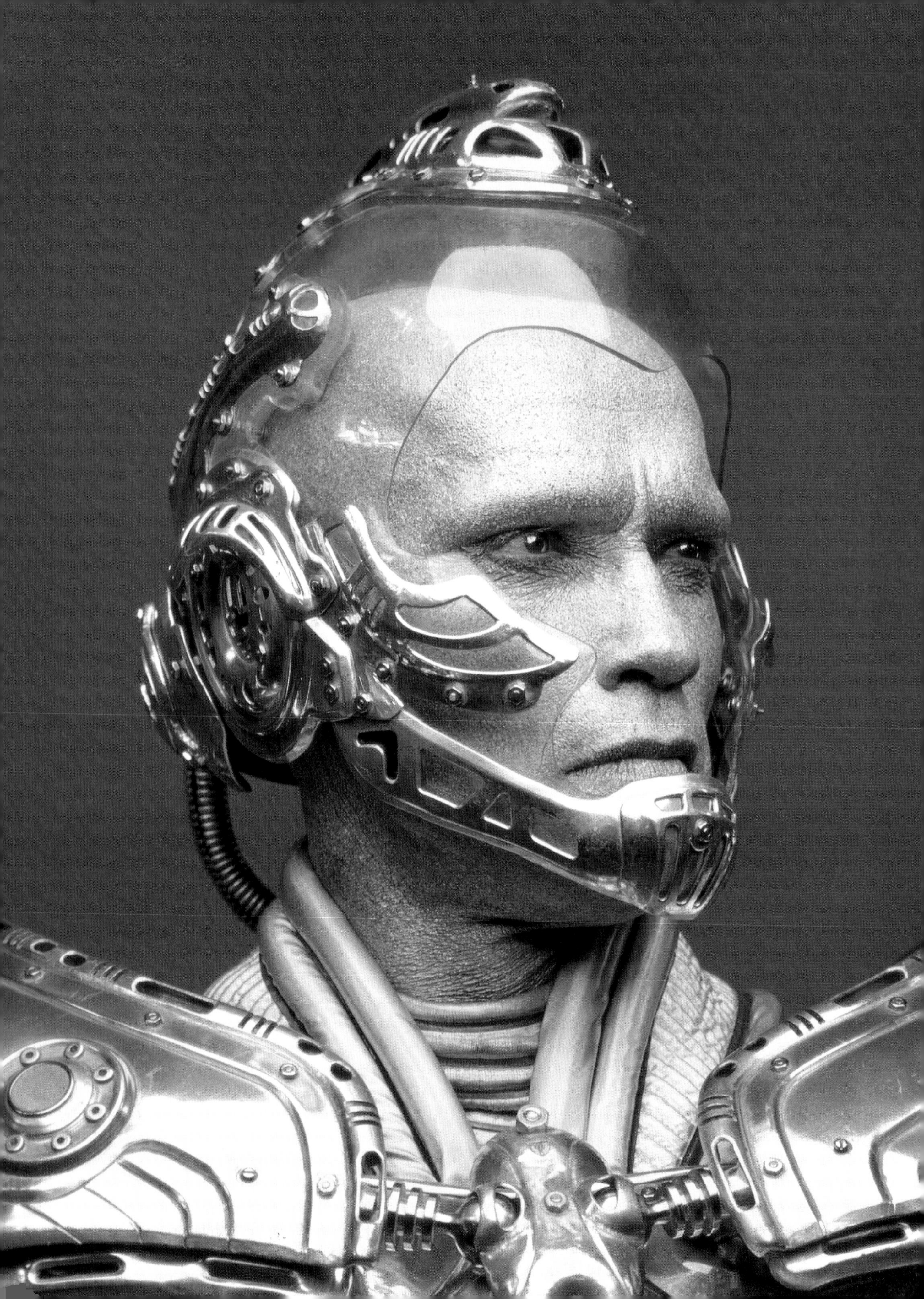

MR. FREEZE

"A Time to Freeze!" Joel Schumacher exclaims upon the first on-set arrival of Arnold Schwarzenegger, magnificently displayed in arch-villainous regalia on the Gotham Observatory set at the Long Beach Seaport Dome. Members of the crew cannot help but ooh and aah over Schwarzenegger in Mr. Freeze's gleaming suit of futuristic armor, with its cool blue lights and matching helmet.

Schumacher walks over to Schwarzenegger and raps on the heavy suit. "Do you know the difference between wearing this and just feeling it?" asks Schwarzenegger in his mock-challenging, joking mode. "Well," ripostes the director, "I guess it's hard to feel when you're wearing a *Buick*!"

There was good cause for celebration. Schwarzenegger is more than a movie star...he's a bona fide international icon, and his participation in the film can only boost his already mighty reputation.

Driven by an unquenchable desire to succeed against all odds, Schwarzenegger conquered first the highly competitive world of bodybuilding, then Hollywood itself, rising to the highest ranks of motion picture luminaries through a combination of sheer determination, tremendous professional discipline and an uncanny ability to choose the road best traveled. Add to this a brilliant business acumen—among his pursuits, Schwarzenegger is successful in the real estate and gym businesses, and is one of the team behind the monumentally thriving Planet Hollywood theme restaurants located around the world—and a terrific family (Schwarzenegger is married to television journalist Maria Shriver, with whom he has three children), and you have one truly meaningful life.

ARNOLD SCHWARZENEGGER

What has made this man so attractive to audiences around the world? For one thing, Schwarzenegger is a man who's always *thinking* about the world. His mentality operates on a global basis, carefully choosing his projects based on their international appeal. "Perhaps it's because I am from overseas," he says, "because when I read a script one of the first questions I ask myself is whether the movie is for the entire world. For some, perhaps, Italy or Germany or Japan or Brazil may be nice places to take a vacation. For me, these are important markets with audiences seeking entertainment, just as Americans do."

Schwarzenegger is more than a great action hero...he's also a gifted comic actor who has been unafraid from the earliest days of his career to kid his own image as a macho man of steel. Humor has always been an important element of Schwarzenegger's "straight" roles, but several of his films are unabashed comedies.

As Mr. Freeze, Schwarzenegger welds liberal doses of humor with a moving portrayal of a tormented man turned to twisted deeds by grief and loneliness. This potent combination proved to be attractive to Schwarzenegger, who can afford to be highly selective about the parts he chooses.

Schwarzenegger takes some time to muse about his *Batman & Robin* work during one of his two-and-a-half-hour makeup sessions. "The villains of the *Batman* comics, TV show and movies have always been fantastically colorful, bizarre and entertaining characters," Schwarzenegger

notes. "Villains are fun to play, because you can dig as deep as you can inside of yourself to find whatever evil is there, and then play with it. Joel Schumacher is a very talented director who can really get to you and pull out the best performance."

Schwarzenegger admits that when Schumacher approached him about the possibility of his playing Mr. Freeze, "Obviously, it was the last thing I ever thought of. But Joel and I had often talked about the possibility of working together, and it seemed to be an interesting opportunity."

Schwarzenegger's research began immediately. "I studied the comic books that featured Mr. Freeze and also looked at the way he was played by Otto Preminger, George Sanders and Eli Wallach on the TV series. Then I had to figure out how to separate my Mr. Freeze from theirs, and how to make it memorable within the context of all the other terrific *Batman* villains. Because, you know, these movies are going to go on forever, and after people see *Batman X*, they'll look back and talk about their favorite villains."

Following his discussions with Schumacher about the character concept, "I got really excited by it," declares Schwarzenegger. "In *Batman & Robin*, you have the action and the comedy. Also, Mr. Freeze is a villain with strongly sympathetic overtones, which makes him even more interesting to play. After all, he's basically motivated by tremendous love for his wife, whom he was unable to cure of McGregor's Syndrome. Anyone who has suffered such loss—or has even imagined it—can perhaps understand why Dr. Victor Fries would go crazy."

Schwarzenegger was enthusiastic about sharing the screen with such a powerhouse cast. "That's one of the great things about *Batman* movies...you don't feel like you have to carry the movie alone. Instead, 10 great actors will collectively carry the film. Joel has a knack for bringing together really wonderful performers, which brings your own level of performance up."

Schwarzenegger has continually been bringing his "level of performance up" since his motion picture debut 25 years ago. But there was a whole other life before he stepped in front of the camera. As a child in Graz, Austria, Schwarzenegger was encouraged by his father to become involved in athletics. At 15, he discovered his genuine passion, weightlifting, which led to bodybuilding. At the age of 20, Schwarzenegger became Mr. Universe.

Schwarzenegger's movie career began with the critically acclaimed *Pumping Iron*, a documentary about the Mr. Universe competition. Director Bob Rafelson, recogniz-

ing Schwarzenegger's engaging natural presence before the camera, cast him in *Stay Hungry*. Raves from performance in hand, in 1978 he put aside bodybuilding to pursue acting full-time.

Schwarzenegger's breakthrough role was in *Conan the Barbarian*. The film spawned a sequel and earned Schwarzenegger a devoted following. He next took a chance on a low-budget independent film by an unknown director. James Cameron's futuristic thriller *The Terminator*, released in 1984, became a runaway hit at the box office.

Over the next few years, Schwarzenegger became virtually synonymous with the phrase "action hero," largely due to the phenomenal success of a series of action-adventure films. But, in 1988, Schwarzenegger showcased his untapped talents as a comic actor in *Twins*. That film's success paved the way for more comedies: *Junior, Kindergarten Cop* and *Jingle all the Way*.

Schwarzenegger's greatest commercial success to date came with *Terminator 2: Judgment Day*, which reunited him with Cameron. His other recent films include *Total Recall, Last Action Hero, True Lies,* and *Eraser*. Schwarzenegger made his directorial debut in 1990 on "The Switch," an episode of the popular series *Tales from the Crypt*. He also directed a remake of the holiday classic *Christmas in Connecticut*, for TNT.

Meanwhile, Schwarzenegger has tirelessly worked for the well-being of young people around the country. Over the years, he has served as the weight training coach for the Special Olympics, Executive Commissioner of the Los Angeles Inner-City Games, chairman of the National Inner-City Games Foundation, and on the President's Council on Physical Fitness and Sports.

On the set, Schwarzenegger was unfailingly affable, more than living up to his professional standing and his well-deserved reputation for one-liners. Considering the physical load he was carrying, this was perhaps one of the actor's most heroic feats. "The costume limits you because you can only move so much under the heavy armor," he says. "You move differently, like a big truck moves differently than a Porsche.

"But," Schwarzenegger smiles with a gleam in his eye, "a big truck can still move *very* fast."

As if to prove that point, makeup completed, the big man glides effortlessly out of his chair and strides purposefully toward the soundstage, where Arnold Schwarzenegger will once more transform himself into Mr. Freeze—and infectiously enjoy every single minute of it.

BATMAN

GEORGE CLOONEY

It's January 1997, just outside of the Seaport Dome in Long Beach. George Clooney has been working seven-day weeks for five months, but those circles around his eyes aren't from fatigue... they're part of the makeup he wears as Batman to accentuate the effect of the blue-black cowl. On this night, hours away from completing his role, Clooney removes the black makeup himself, as he always does, in the trailer that's been his home-away-from-home-away-from-home (since he has yet *another* trailer back on the Warner Bros. set of *ER* in Burbank).

"Doing *Batman & Robin* was more fun than I ever thought," states Clooney. "The crew, better than I ever thought. The cast, nicer than I ever thought. I was a little bit intimidated by working with such a giant group of people on a production of this size. I recall standing on a tremendous set on one of my first days of shooting, and telling Joel Schumacher that I felt a little out of my league. And Joel said, 'So do we all. This is the biggest thing any of us will ever do, so just enjoy it.'"

George Clooney is the third actor since 1989 to essay the role of billionaire philanthropist Bruce Wayne and his immortal *alter ego*, Batman. Once again, the series is freshened by another version of a character whose endurance has, to a great degree, been predicated upon his varied interpretations by a talented parade of artists, writers, cartoonists and actors.

Clooney wanted to portray a Batman/ Bruce Wayne more at ease with his dual role in the world and less inclined to garment-rending and breast-beating—in other words, to play a Caped Crusader not unlike the traditional DC Comics character, in a way that to some extent reflects his own life. "Batman and I actually have a lot in common," he says with a sidelong smile. "We both actually have rather good lives. We both make a very good living, we're both bachelors and we're both not unpopular.

"The truth of the matter," Clooney continues, "is that although I'm working seven days a week right now, which is very difficult, no one wants to hear me complain. So I don't, and that's fair enough, because my life is also a very good one. By the same token, we have now seen three *Batman* films in which he talks about how his parents were murdered when he was a little

boy, and the truth is that people now want this man to stop talking about it already!

"It's time for Batman to enjoy being Batman, and deal with the problems at hand rather than the problems of his past. But that doesn't mean that he's not frustrated by the criminals who roam around Gotham, or that he doesn't still have some issues of his own to deal with."

Clooney's directness, great sense of humor and utter lack of pretension endeared him to all in the *Batman & Robin* company, and he often had the company in stitches. Example: wearing the magnificent advanced armored Batsuit while standing on the platform in the climactic Gotham Observatory sequence, the irrepressible Clooney thrusts up his hands and intones, "I am not a crook" in the familiar physical and vocal stylings of President Richard Nixon. A few moments later, Joel Schumacher stages the scene in which Robin and Batgirl have plummeted off of a telescope to what seems to be a certain death thousands of feet below. Before the camera rolls, Clooney plays his own bent version of the sequence. "Good-bye, kids," Clooney waves casually to the descending twosome. "No more Robin! No more Batgirl! Now it's mine, all mine!," followed by a cackling laugh worthy of Snidely Whiplash. (Of course, when Schumacher calls, "Action," it's back to Batman basics.)

Then there are Clooney's famous lunchtime pickup basketball games, playing with such Warner Bros. pals as *Lois and Clark's* Dean Cain (imagine that...Batman and Superman on the same court), *ER's* Eriq La Salle, hair stylist Waldo Sanchez and, quite often, his *Batman & Robin* colleague Chris O'Donnell. Toward the end of production, Clooney came down hard on the court, badly spraining his ankle and tearing some ligaments, which had him working through considerable pain in the last two weeks of shooting. "I was trying to prove that white men *can* jump," he joked afterward. "They just don't know how to *land*."

Clooney uses humor to break the natural tension of the often laborious filmmaking process. But he's also been a seriously hard-working actor for 15 years, since moving to Los Angeles from his native Kentucky. Although he is the son of American Movie Classics network host Nick Clooney, the nephew of singer Rosemary Clooney and the cousin of actor Miguel Ferrer, he spent his first year in Hollywood unemployed. For over a decade, he paid his dues in grade C features, dead-end TV shows and pilots that didn't get picked up.

Now, however—since emerging as one of the stars of the ensemble cast of *ER*—Clooney's career has kicked into overdrive. He's earned Emmy, Screen Actors Guild, Golden Globe and People's Choice nominations.

His fortunes in features have improved, too. His charged performance as a bad-ass bank robber battling border-town vampires in Robert Rodriguez's *From Dusk Till Dawn* turned heads. He followed this by starring opposite Michelle Pfeiffer in the romantic comedy *One Fine Day*, and will be seen this fall opposite Nicole Kidman in the action-thriller *The Peacemaker*.

Growing up, Clooney was a big fan of the *Batman* TV series, but admits that "I wasn't a big comic-book guy. Where we grew up, television was everything, and *Batman* was our favorite show. My cousin Miguel Ferrer used to make plaster statuettes of Batman and give them to everybody as gifts."

No one was more surprised than Clooney when Joel Schumacher asked him to don the mantle of the Dark Knight. "It sounded great, and I really wanted to work with Joel. I had also been over at Warner Bros. for a long time on *ER*, and there's really a nice sense of family that doesn't exist anywhere else in Hollywood. The idea of being able to work on the biggest franchise of all time thrilled me, and we made the deal."

Ultimately, what does Clooney hope to add to the 60-year-long mythology of *Batman*? "We'll see when it's done, because I can never tell what I'm putting on film while I'm doing it," he responds with typical modesty. "First and foremost, I don't want to screw up what has already worked so well. It's the most successful movie franchise ever, so I'm not trying to make this thing 'right.' You try and do it differently, but you don't want to be different just to be different. There are certain things that you have to uphold when playing a character like Batman.

"The secret to Batman," offers Clooney, "is that he's kind of the Johnny Carson of super heroes. The reason Carson was such a great host was not only that he was funny and warm and we really liked him, but he also always made sure that the guest was the star. The truth of the matter is that the star of this movie is not Batman. The criminals are always the star, because they're so much bigger than life. Batman is the constant, the steady in this. So my job is to be the foundation to hold all this together, because in a way the audience watches the movie through Batman's eyes.

"Hopefully, the stars are the wild characters, the sets, the costumes, the wonderful camerawork. It's an epic! My task is not to try and grab the attention all the time."

Nevertheless, Clooney must know that there's little way to escape the extraordinary amount of attention that comes with this role. And thus, the big question...how do you top this?

"Well, you don't top it," he responds. "You just do something different. Playing Batman is a high point in my career, so I'm very happy to do it because the older you get, the more you realize that it all comes down to just enjoying what you do. On this movie, I got to spend six months out of my life truly enjoying my life. As an actor, you have to love the entire process. If you're auditioning, you have to love the auditioning process. You have to love the casting process. You have to love the publicity process.

"You have to love it all," Clooney concludes. "Because otherwise...you shouldn't be there!"

ROBIN

Enjoying a break during camera setups, Chris O'Donnell relaxes on the carpeted floor of his trailer on the Warner Bros. lot. "Lots of repeaters on this *Batman* movie from the last one," muses O'Donnell. "I guess the newcomers are in the minority. But that's great, because it takes a lot of the pressure off."

It's hard to believe that O'Donnell ever feels any pressure at all, since he always projects confidence, assurance, and absolutely no arrogance. Cleaving to his Midwestern roots, his family and childhood friends, he seems incapable of ever "going Hollywood," even though he's now one of Tinseltown's favorite young actors.

Although O'Donnell starred in two major films since *Batman Forever—The Chamber* and *In Love and War*—he was eager to roar back into Gotham. "I've never done a sequel before," the actor notes. "It feels very comfortable coming back, there's lots of friendly faces and you know the routine."

One new face was, of course, George Clooney. And it was soon clear that the chemistry between the two was exactly right for their characters. When they're in the same place at the same time, Clooney and O'Donnell are a pair of wits who just won't quit.

O'Donnell was pleased to find himself relating well to the new Caped Crusader. "I thought that Val Kilmer did a great job," he says, "but as long as Joel had to cast a new Batman, I'm glad he chose George. He's great in the role, and we have a lot in common. He's also addicted to basketball and golf, and he's famous for kidding around on the set."

But art does not always imitate life. "One of the interesting things about the

CHRIS O'DONNELL

movie," explains O'Donnell, "is that there has been development in the relationship between Dick and Bruce. Dick has grown tired of living in Bruce's shadows. It's still kind of Batman's show, and Dick is thinking that he deserves a little more of the credit and attention. He's doing his share of the crime fighting as Robin, but feels like Batman doesn't treat him as an equal. So Dick is starting to get a little restless."

The actor first came to prominence as Jessica Lange's son in *Men Don't Leave*, following with roles in *Fried Green Tomatoes, School Ties* and *Blue Sky*. At the age of 21, his role opposite Al Pacino in *Scent of a Woman* merited a Golden Globe nomination. He was next seen in *The Three Musketeers, Circle of Friends* and *Mad Love*.

As O'Donnell's reputation has grown, has returning to the Batcave been a pleasure or a challenge? "From an acting standpoint, it's pure fun," says O'Donnell. "It's good to take a break from serious dramatic films and play around a little. It's challenging in a different way. I appreciate the whole process of making films, and it's great to sit back and watch a movie like *Batman & Robin* being made. And from a professional standpoint, this is my bread and butter. So obviously I wanted to go back and do it again!"

And with that, O'Donnell rises from the trailer floor and sprints off to don the fabulously designed heavy latex Robin suit and to once again make that character his very own.

POISON IVY

UMA THURMAN

"Star-crossed lovers separated by temperature" is how Uma Thurman describes the relationship between her Poison Ivy and Arnold Schwarzenegger's Mr. Freeze. This cool phrase reveals the actress's fundamental intelligence and sense of humor. Add to those characteristics a jolt of staggering beauty, and you have the reason that Uma Thurman is one of the most sought-after leading women in film today.

In *Batman & Robin*, Thurman essays the dual sides of the toxically splendiferous Poison Ivy and the geeky Pamela Isley with a flair that knowingly winks at past screen *femmes fatales* while making her creation alternately terrifying, touching and hilarious. Just listen to the way Thurman injects even so simple a line as "Hi there" with a come-hither, insouciant detachment that tickles and intrigues.

A dedicated professional, Thurman astutely sized up her character. "She's very loquacious," she notes. "She's basically a talker, a manipulator and a hustler." The actress worked closely with her director and screenwriter to evolve the character. "Every movie is about the process, about scratching away and slowly inhabiting the role. For Poison Ivy, it was about refinement and, hopefully, bringing me to life in the role."

The daughter of Dr. Robert Thurman—the famed scholar of Tibetan Buddhism—Uma was discovered at 15 by two agents in a New England prep school play. She then transferred to the Professional Children's School in New York. In 1986, she made her screen debut at the age of 16 in a small role in the low-budget *Kiss Daddy Goodnight*, then appeared in *Johnny Be Good*.

But it was with her dual role as the goddess Venus and the nerdy Rose in Terry Gilliam's fantasy *The Adventures of Baron Munchausen* that Thurman made her mark.

From this point on, she would demonstrate versatility, fearlessness in her choice of material and a staunch resistance to treading footworn highways of easy success, as her credits prove. Among her subsequent films are *Dangerous Liaisons*, *Henry and June*, *Mad Dog and Glory*, and *Even Cowgirls Get the Blues*. In 1994, Thurman starred with John Travolta in Quentin Tarantino's *Pulp Fiction*, earning her an Oscar nomination. She has since appeared in *A Month by the Lake*, *Beautiful Girls* and *The Truth About Cats and Dogs*.

Except for *Baron Munchausen*, none of Thurman's films can be considered epic in scale, and she had to become comfortable with *Batman & Robin*'s sheer size. "In the beginning it was very nerve-racking," she admits, "but because of this difference, it's also been fascinating.

"The bottom line," Thurman concludes, "is that this is a comic-book world, so everybody keeps it light and fun, which is just as it should be."

BATGIRL

ALICIA SILVERSTONE

In conceiving *Batman & Robin*, Joel Schumacher and writer Akiva Goldsman realized that while boys have always had action heroes to identify with, girls have fewer heroines to follow. However, since the multimedia evolution of the Caped Crusader had already provided a young heroine in Batgirl, they decided to revive her character.

There are few actresses of her generation as much on the cutting edge as Alicia Silverstone. After she made her debut in *The Crush*, Silverstone catapulted to worldwide success in Amy Heckerling's critical and box-office smash *Clueless*.

As strikingly serious and self-possessed as she is radiantly beautiful, Silverstone recalls the invitation from Schumacher to portray Batgirl. "I was in Japan on a press tour for *Clueless* when Joel called me from Mississippi, where he was filming *A Time to Kill*. I could barely hear him, but I was thrilled."

Silverstone became a *Batman* fan via reruns of the ABC series. "I watched them when I was a little girl and loved the characters, especially Catwoman and the Joker." She was delighted, though, that Schumacher was asking her to play a positive character, rather than a villain. "I think it's really nice that with Batgirl, there's a high-profile action star who's female," says Silverstone. "It's wonderful that now little girls, too, can have someone to look up to."

The 20-year-old actress was born and raised in San Francisco. Not long after attending her first acting workshop at the age of 13, she was spotted by an agent. Guest shots on *The Wonder Years* and roles in the telefilms *Torch Song* and *Scattered Dreams* soon followed.

She has added many more credits to her growing résumé, including the cable movie *The Cool and the Crazy* and the features *Hideaway*, *The Babysitter*, *True Crime* and *Le Nouveau Monde*, as well as the three Aerosmith videos that made her one of MTV's favorite young stars. Just previous to *Batman & Robin*, Silverstone produced and starred in *Excess Baggage*, the first of two films under a deal between Columbia Pictures and her company, First Kiss.

On the set, Silverstone forged a close "uncle/niece" bond with Michael Gough. "I love Michael," she says with great warmth. "He's such a delight to be around and constantly makes me laugh. Michael is so kind, and a true gentleman."

As for the other two members of Gotham's dynamic trio, Silverstone breaks out in an incandescent smile. "George is very kind, and when he and Chris get together they're a comedy team that helps make wearing the Batgirl suit more comfortable."

Ultimately, as both a young star and producer, Silverstone hopes "to learn as much as I can about everything I'm interested in." Considering what she's already accomplished, audiences will be happy to continue the journey with her.

ALFRED PENNYWORTH

MICHAEL GOUGH

There is a myth afoot that Michael Gough and Alfred Pennyworth—that is, the great British actor and the impeccable butler that he portrays for the fourth time in *Batman & Robin*—are nearly interchangeable in manner (extraordinarily polite and kind), bearing (remarkably distinguished) and countenance (incredibly dashing). And all of the above is true... except that Gough is also graced with a hilariously irreverent and sometimes even outrageous wit that deflates any hint of pretension, in either himself or others.

In other words, Michael Gough is *not* Alfred...well, not *exactly*.

"I'm delighted to hear that," the actor asserts at the end of a long day of filming in Long Beach, "because I do try to find, and then develop, the character of Alfred as someone quite separate from myself.

"I think what's interesting about this particular film is that you see what an immensely caring person Bruce Wayne really is. Alfred loves Bruce not because he's his boss, but because he's a wonderful person to work *with* rather than *for*. He raised Bruce from the time he was a lad to become the kind of person he wants him to be."

Gough, who turned 80 years young during the filming of *Batman & Robin*, has the energy and wit of a man at least half that age. Portraying Alfred each time in the *Batman* features, Gough's participation has become nearly as crucial an element in these four films as the Caped Crusader's himself. And he never would have done it if he hadn't liked Alfred Pennyworth in the first place.

"I think he's a very honest, honorable man and all his sharpness has nothing to do with me at all," Gough says with a self-deprecating smile. "That comes from somewhere else. But I think he really is a lovely character."

Throughout the lengthy shoot of *Batman & Robin*—and his entire career, for that matter—Gough has always maintained his own power of positive thinking about his art, proud to be a working actor, his enthusiasm never flagging, his bright spirit always cheering his co-workers. "I think we're very lucky to be actors," he declares. "The truth is what we're after. What we're trying to do is to get as close to the character we're playing as possible, and I think we can...by being truthful.

"I have been earning my living for 60 years by acting and been able to pay the rent and bring up the children and grandchildren," Gough concludes. "I've done everything that comes up, and if I'm out of work and they want me to be the back end of a donkey at the pantomime, then that's what I'll do. But I do want to be the best, to be as good as I possibly can and make it as real as I can. That's the challenge. That's the excitement!"

COMMISSIONER GORDON

PAT HINGLE

Now in his fifth decade of professional acting, Pat Hingle for the fourth time brings his enormous skills to the role of Gotham's Police Commissioner Gordon in *Batman & Robin*. It just wouldn't feel like a *Batman* film without Hingle's presence; his relatively brief appearances as Gordon link each film to the other in a very tangible manner. On his first day of work at Warner Bros. Studios, decked out in Gordon's impressive, dark-blue dress uniform, Hingle received more stares from passers-by than the comparatively low-key nature of the role might suggest.

Curiously enough, Hingle has always based Commissioner Gordon emotionally on a scene that, although scripted for the first *Batman* film, was never shot. "In the initial *Batman*," Hingle recollects on a walk from the set to the Warner Bros. Commissary for his lunch break, "Gordon was just a cop on the beat and, after hearing the gunshots, was the first one at the scene of the murder of young Bruce Wayne's parents. He finds this little boy, crying over his dead mother and father, and the next day the Gotham newspaper runs a photograph of this kid clinging on to Gordon, who is trying to console him.

"That's why," Hingle notes, "every time I look at Bruce Wayne, what I'm trying to say with my eyes is, 'Do you recognize me yet, guy?'"

That scripted incident was, in fact, one of two reasons Hingle accepted the role of Commissioner Gordon in the first place, although when it was excised he accepted it with his usual professional aplomb. "The other reason," he admits with a conspiratorial chuckle, "was because my wife, Julie, had never been to London, where we shot the first *Batman*, and I wanted to spend some time with her there.

"Gordon is really kind of a bit part in the films," Hingle continues, "but I certainly don't approach him that way. I know so much more about the Commissioner than there is on film. What a straight-shooter he is. How many times crooked politicians have tried to get to him, and failed. But I feel sorry for Gordon, because without Batman and Robin to help him, he'd be in trouble.

"Somehow," he laughs, "the Gotham police are always screwing up in one way or another."

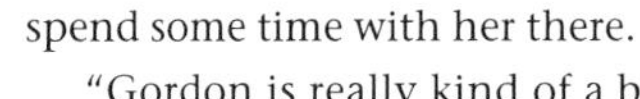

JULIE MADISON

ELLE MACPHERSON

The stupendously beautiful Elle Macpherson has successfully made the transition from one of the world's most famous models to a busy film actress, choosing her roles carefully. She made her motion picture debut in 1994 with Hugh Grant in John Duigan's much lauded *Sirens* and subsequently played in Franco Zeffirelli's *Jane Eyre*, the romantic comedy *If Lucy Fell* and Barbra Streisand's *The Mirror Has Two Faces*.

Simultaneously with filming her role in *Batman & Robin* as Bruce Wayne's beautiful but frustrated fiancée, Julie Madison, Macpherson was starring in her biggest part yet, commuting to Alberta, Canada, to appear opposite Anthony Hopkins and Alec Baldwin in the David Mamet thriller *Bookworm*.

Julie Madison is a character with some real history behind her. She was created in the early *Batman* comic books as Bruce Wayne's high-society fiancée, who ultimately drops the elusive billionaire because of his playboy ways. In *Batman & Robin*, Julie is one of the few characters who has just one personality rather than two and, as such, is anchored by a recognizable gravity. This was exactly why Macpherson was so intrigued to play her.

"I just thought it was nice, coming from a larger-than-life background like the fashion world," she remarks, "to finally play a character who *isn't*. I'm able to draw upon the sensuality that's part of what I do in fashion, but take it to a more realistic depth.

"Julie is intelligent, well educated, and kind of a grounding force," adds Macpherson. "You have to believe the relationship that she's had with Bruce Wayne, which is finally a very frustrating one for her."

Growing up in Australia, Macpherson was quite familiar with the legend and lore of Batman. "I was raised with the comics and television show, and it's just wonderful to see how it's evolved under Joel's direction. I love the sensuality and dry sense of humor of his vision, as opposed to the slapstick and camp of the TV version. Ultimately, it's romantic, and a pleasure to be involved with."

JASON WOODRUE

JOHN GLOVER

John Glover wistfully peers out across Long Beach Harbor. Before him lies the old and new hotels, convention centers and office buildings on the opposite side from the port that contains the antiquarian bulk of the *Queen Mary*, as well as the Long Beach Seaport Dome right next door, where he's nearly completed his final scenes in *Batman & Robin*.

"I'm just standing here mourning," says Glover with an edge of melodramatic humor. "It's my last day and it's just too soon for Woody to disappear."

"Woody" is Glover's own affectionate term for the remarkably unlovable Dr. Jason Woodrue, the wicked and very mad scientist whose lustful designs on his colleague Pamela Isley (Uma Thurman) result in her terrible transformation into Poison Ivy...followed by his own dreadful demise after receiving her first lethal kiss.

Glover's talents were well-known to Joel Schumacher, ever since the two worked together on *The Incredible Shrinking Woman*—the director's first feature effort—more than 15 years before they reunited on *Batman & Robin*. "Joel simply explained to me what Dr. Woodrue was going to be in the film, and that he hoped I would consider doing it," recalls Glover. "And when he told me that I would get kissed to death by Uma Thurman in the end...I thought, 'Well, why not?'"

Ironically, Glover was by no means a fan of the *Batman* films, nor familiar with Dr. Jason Woodrue's DC Comics history, when he was approached by Schumacher. "You can say that ignorance is bliss, 'tis folly to be wise," the actor laughs. "Because when I came to start work, I wasn't exactly sure what to expect. Then they put these great glasses on my head, an unbelievable wig, and then rubber gloves and lab coat, so I just kind of jumped into it all. Who knows what I would have come up with if I'd had pre-knowledge of who I was supposed to be?"

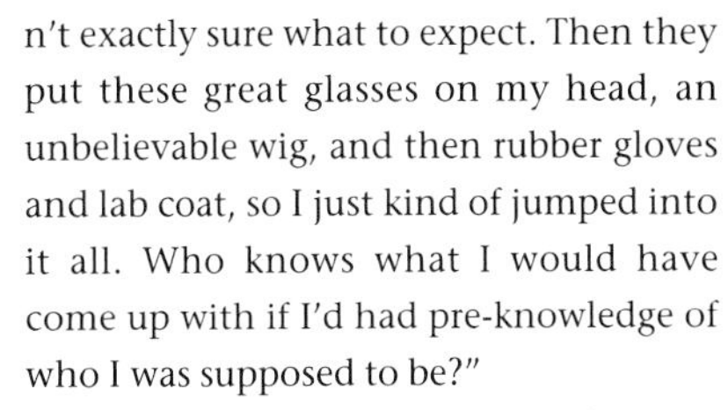

And what does John Glover take away from playing mad, bad and dangerous-to-know Dr. Woodrue on this balmy fall day? "The lesson of letting go. Of just trusting my instincts, and sense of *joie*. That, and trusting that Joel won't allow me to make a fool of myself!"

BANE

So that no one confuses the reel with the real, let's visit Jeep Swenson, the monumentally proportioned actor (6'4", 400 lbs.) who portrays the scientifically fabricated, all-purpose weapon of destruction dubbed Bane in his dressing room trailer. With his character's mask removed, revealing a friendly face, Swenson takes a short swig of water, then discusses Bane's relationship with his "owner," Poison Ivy. "It's almost like the relationship between George and Lenny in *Of Mice and Men*," muses Swenson thoughtfully, "with the more diminutive person taking charge and telling the bigger one how to think."

JEEP SWENSON

Hold on a second! Bane discussing John Steinbeck? Of course. Jeep Swenson defies typecasting; he's the quintessential gentle giant, and the fact that he can screw your head off with a flick of his wrist is utterly besides the point. "Everybody thinks of big muscle guys as dopes or narcissistic idiots," he says in a soft drawl. "But I was a smart man before I was big. I graduated from the University of Texas with a 3.65 average."

After college the San Antonio native, who then weighed only 170 pounds, became a professional rodeo cowboy. When Swenson's shoulder was badly injured in a rodeo mishap, an orthopedic surgeon suggested weight lifting to rebuild those muscles.

"I gained 100 pounds in one year," he recalls. "No steroids, just eating, sleeping, training. It knocked me right out of rodeo." He moved on to professional wrestling. Known as Jeep the Mercenary, he's bested opponents like The Ultimate Warrior and Hulk Hogan. "I didn't so much 'beat him' as 'beat him up,'" Jeep says of his encounter with the latter. However, the two adversaries became friendly enough to share a movie set when Swenson made his film debut in *No Holds Barred*. "But I hated it," admits Swenson. "I complained the whole time. Then I got involved with *Walker, Texas Ranger*, which lit a fire in me. Suddenly, acting became a passion."

When Swenson met Joel Schumacher about *Batman & Robin*, "he showed me Bane in the *Batman* comic book and said, 'This is what you're going to be doing.' I just got the part right off the bat."

Swenson doesn't complain that he's obscured by Bane's mask throughout *Batman & Robin*, or that his "dialogue" is grunts and growls, or that his entire body was icily spray-painted in a daily three-hour makeup session. He knows that people will know who he is and who he played. "The simple fact is that when the other actors get out of their costumes, they become Arnold Schwarzenegger, George Clooney, and so on. But when I take my Bane outfit off, I'm still 400 pounds of muscle, and that's what really draws people, especially young ones. Kids want to see a bigger-than-life action figure."

MS. B. HAVEN & NORA FRIES

VIVICA A. FOX

1996 was quite a year for Vivica A. Fox, who gave Hollywood a swift kick in the can with her punchy performance in that worldwide phenomenon called *Independence Day*—portraying strong-willed single mother and exotic dancer Jasmine Dubrow—and as one of a quartet of female bank robbers in the powerful *Set It Off*. She has since completed roles in *Good to Go, Booty Call* and *Soul Food*.

Although Ms. B. Haven was just a one-day cameo for Fox, it amply demonstrates the actress's range even beyond *Independence Day*, allowing her to incorporate sexiness, sauciness and a comedic flair in her frustrated come-on to the ever-reluctant Freeze. It was these very qualities, plus a very convincing invitation from Joel Schumacher, that excited Fox about joining the *Batman & Robin* team.

"Joel said that he would make me beautiful, and that I could just have a good time and be a ham, 'cause everyone else was," recollects Fox with an earthy laugh.

So in she came, in the midst of a massive cast and crew that had already known one another for months, to play one crucial and entertaining scene with Arnold Schwarzenegger, one of the most famous men in the world. "You either stepped up to the plate or got run over," Fox notes matter-of-factly.

VENDELA THOMMESSEN

Supermodel Vendela Thommessen makes her motion picture debut in the role of Nora, the loving wife whose degenerative illness provides Arnold Schwarzenegger's Dr. Victor Fries with his *raison d'être* to go mad in his search for a cure while he keeps her cryogenically frozen.

Vendela had entertained several feature film offers before Joel Schumacher approached her to portray Nora, "but I was trying to just work hard in my acting class," she reflects after her first day on the set. "I think some people making a transition from one part of the profession to the other accept a large part before they're capable of handling it. I thought starting out little by little was a better idea. And the way Joel described the emotional tie between Nora and Victor, it felt like there was something that could affect the entire film."

Although Vendela knew about Batman while growing up in Sweden, it wasn't until she moved to the United States that she realized how big the character really is. "It was sort of the same thing as when I did the *Sports Illustrated* swimsuit covers. In my country it was no big thing, just another issue of a popular magazine. All of a sudden, people would tell me, 'Hey Vendela, you looked great in Alaska,' or whatever. Maybe *Batman & Robin* will have the same effect."

GOTHAM DELUXE

When the sets of a film become a must-see on the celebrity circuit, you know that something unusual is going on...and if the parade of famous faces that appeared on the *Batman & Robin* set was any indication, the new Gotham City that arose on five soundstages at Warner Bros., the Long Beach Seaport Dome, the miniatures facility deep in the San Fernando Valley and elsewhere was the best show in town.

It was production designer Barbara Ling's statement to Joel Schumacher when asked if they had another *Batman* movie in them—"We haven't even scratched the surface"—that helped to encourage the filmmaker to once again take the plunge into Gotham City and its inhabitants. In fact, Ling and Schumacher have more than scratched the surface—they've dug their nails in deep, uncovering treasures in their wake.

Ling, who in addition to *Batman Forever* has such films on her résumé as *The Doors, Fried Green Tomatoes* and Schumacher's *Falling Down*, was charged to reveal anew—rather than repeat—in all the areas under her jurisdiction: sets, vehicles and gadgetry. This is a woman who truly deserves her job description of "production designer."

Ling had only five months off between the completion of her work on *Batman Forever* and beginning labor on *Batman & Robin*, so she didn't linger in the "real" world very long before diving back into the glorious extremities of Gotham City. Nearly a year before principal photography started in September 1996, Ling began to assemble a crew for the mighty task ahead: illustrators, model makers, set designers, sculptors, storyboard artists, and so on. Hammering her fabulous concepts into reality were construction coordinator Greg Callas and his associate Rich Hoffenberg, already richly experienced from serving in the same capacities on both *Batman Returns* and *Batman Forever*.

The rest of the art department crew assembled by Barbara Ling contained an enormous number of talented artists, recognized as the best in their respective fields. Just some of these people are: supervising art director Richard Holland; art directors James Hegedus and Geoff Hubbard; assistant art directors Charlie Daboub and John Marshall; digital art director Lance Hammer; senior set designers Richard Berger and James Bayliss, heading a veritable army of set designers, among them Stella Furner (who appropriately describes her team's contributions by saying, "We are the ones *behind* the behind-the-scenes"), B. Gilbert Clayton, Keith Cunningham, Eric D. Sundahl, Gary Speckman, Stan Tropp, John Goldsmith, Dawn Brown and John P. Bruce; illustrators Joe Griffith Jr., Patrick Janicke, Tani Kunitake, Mary E. Locatell, Wil Madoc Rees and Jacques Rey; vehicles design illustrator Harald Belker; storyboard artists Raymond Consing and Edwin Natividad; head sculptor Yarek Alfer; art department supervisor Carol Kiefer; and staff assistants Jason A. Mahakian, Daniel Rodriguez-Wolfson and Andy Fink.

"I think this is the biggest film that any of us have ever worked on," says Richard Holland. "Yes, this is sweaty work, but it's also very gratifying."

"*Batman and Robin* outdoes just about anything I've worked on," adds veteran set designer Richard Berger, "including *My Fair Lady*."

Elaborately painted backdrops of Gotham City on Warner Bros. Stage 12 indicate the city's scope and retro-futuristic majesty.

THE CONCEPT OF GOTHAM

In her office perched on the third floor of Warner Bros. Stage 15, Barbara Ling is surrounded by a seemingly chaotic mass of sketches, storyboards, blueprints, books, bulletin boards chock-a-block with photos torn from magazines, set models—all of the influences and results of her magnificent work on *Batman & Robin*.

"For *Batman & Robin*, I wanted to add even more architectural extremes than we did for *Batman Forever*," states Ling. "It's still holding true to the spirit of Russian constructivists, but we wanted to weave in more of an art nouveau feeling.

"This Gotham City is larger than the one seen in *Batman Forever*. The interiors have taken on more of the scope of the exteriors in proportion and size. Probably the biggest difference is that we will have a much greater sense of what the environs of Gotham really look like. You'll see a wider scope of having an inner city, and the excitement of chases across the rooftops of Gotham.

"Gotham has always been for me a combination of everything we know, creating a world that feels familiar, but not enough to put your finger on. It has a size proportion bigger than anything that actually exists, but within those proportions you recognize elements of other histories of architecture and other places. Gotham is a fusion of many cultures and periods of time, but it has no time element. It could be anywhere in time. It's not the future. It's not the past. It's Gotham-time.

"I'm absolutely influenced by the *Batman* comic books. The great sense of how things soar out of frame, of how color washes over something with just a blush of light. The darkened sense of a rich color is more exciting than darkness with no color, which is just bleak. And the comics have always been exciting because of these extraordinary frames that have amazing angles, where buildings are protruding east and west, with swatches of color through them. Gotham is still a dark city, but it's vibrant as well.

"I think the biggest challenge was the icing of the sets. We wanted them to have some translucency, to take ice into a surreal place. We probably did five months of research playing with every kind of toxic and non-toxic material known to man to come up with the right materials for the ice, before discovering a combination fiber resin. It took half a year to make the amount of ice we needed for this movie. The idea was to keep this twinkle about it, ice which feels cold but at the same time could explode because of this inner lighting that is always undulating. We didn't want to just use white ice, and as far as I know, we're the first to come up with this technique."

GOTHAM CITY: BARBARA'S TOUR

The problem with touring the great cities of the world—whether London, Paris, Rome, Kyoto or New York—is that most of their architects and designers are long gone, and one must depend upon contemporary interpreters to explain the whys and wherefores.

But not Gotham! Allow Barbara Ling—articulate, intense, still energized after more than a year of planning, preparation, construction and filming—to take you on her personal tour through the highways and byways of this extraordinary city created and built from ground up in less than a year.

GOTHAM MUSEUM OF NATURAL HISTORY

"The first image that I had when I read the outline of the script was to go after the proportion of what the Field Museum in Chicago felt like when I was a child. I felt like an ant in there, so I wanted to make the Gotham Museum much bigger than a real museum and went after creating a fusion of cultures for the exhibit on display in the great hall. We invented something called 'The Lost World of Tufa,' which squishes together many world cultures from different eras of history—like 20-foot-tall statues of a sphinx body with a Tibetan head, or a Mayan head on top of a Mesopotamian body.

"Architecturally, I always thought it would be interesting to see colonnades of copper and steel, so the museum became a kind of metallized version of the traditional stone-and-concrete institution. We also had to work very closely with the stunt department for the major action sequence in the museum, so we needed enough expanse to create ice floes and ramps for the extreme skaters. The museum had to be functional for the action sequence rather than just something beautiful. Believe it or not, being able to have Yarek Alfer and his sculpture department build the dinosaur statue was crucial, because in any set as large as the museum, you need something to give it a sense of scale when you put a human next to it.

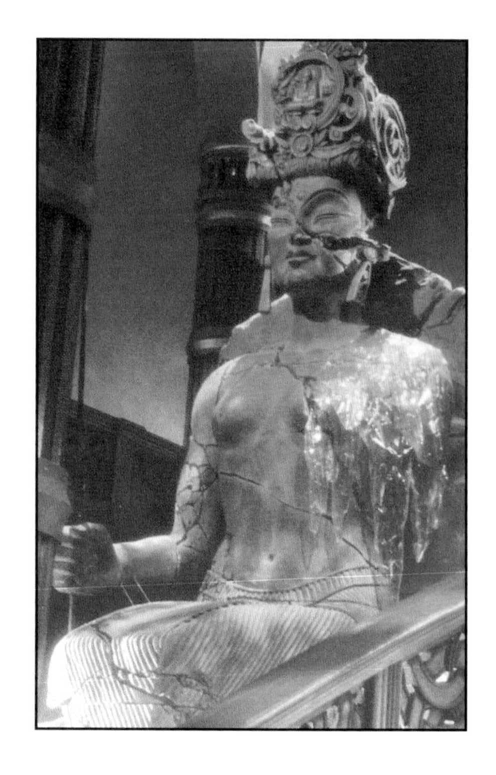

"When the scene in the museum opens, it's already been frozen by Mr. Freeze, and it's the first time the audience gets a sense of this 'Freeze World.' We tried to find a very surreal way to indicate this, and since costume design was play-

Right: *Robin blasts through the double-door entrance of the Gotham Museum on the Redbird.*
Below: *The dinosaur statue and pan-cultural altar in their iced condition.*
Bottom: *The massive Gotham Museum set under construction at Warner Bros. Stage 16.*

ing with reflective materials for the Freeze Suit that were discovered by Jeff Lawrence of the wardrobe department, we worked together to find a similar substance for the floors. I found a cracked Mylar—a film that has a reflective stencil on it—that had a wonderful, iridescent reflective quality. Then we found a clear polyurethane that we could pour onto the floor and create a quarter- to a half-inch surface that could hold up to the extreme cold of the liquid nitrogen that special effects utilizes for the sequence. So we put down Mylar first, almost like wallpaper for the floor, and then poured the urethane, which then hardened into an ice-like substance. When light hits the floor, it refracts back up again, giving you the kind of surreal look we were looking for. This becomes a design motif in the film. Wherever Mr. Freeze goes, the Mylar follows.

"This flooring also worked just fine for the stunt skaters. We had originally laid down an actual 50-by-50-foot ice floor during our tests, but we ironically discovered that ice is ultimately very boring. We could never get a luminous quality out of it, which is why we moved into a *faux* ice format."

The Gotham Museum took five months for Greg Callas, Rich Hoffenberg and their construction crew to build. It stands roughly 60 feet high, 200 feet long and 150 feet wide. The huge skylights that figure in the action weigh over 2000 pounds apiece, and the brachiosaurus statue that meets a cruel fate at the hands of Mr. Freeze rises some 20 feet high.

Right: *The Batmobile on its revolving platform inside the Batcave.*
Below left: *Batman prepares the Batmobile for "takeoff" from its platform.*
Below right: *This illustration indicates Barbara Ling's ambition to create an even more impressive Batcave.*

BATCAVE: NEW AND IMPROVED

"Although I tried to design a much larger Batcave for *Batman Forever*," admits Ling, "on-screen it still translated as smaller than I would have liked. This time, I was determined not to repeat my mistake. The first element of the Batcave I designed was actually the turntable for the Batmobile and the Redbird, which I thought should reflect the Bat-Signal as an enhancement of that visual theme. Just as the Bat-Signal shines in the skies above Gotham, this would be the Bat-Signal deep beneath the surface. The Batmobile surfaces in the middle of this rising Bat-Signal. It became a perfect symbol to have the car positioned on the wings of the Batman emblem as it drives off. Then part of the emblem rises and creates a pod, which splits open and reveals a neon Robin emblem and the Redbird within. The Batmobile turntable in *Batman Forever* was about 20 feet, but to get the Bat Emblem formed on top of it for *Batman & Robin*, I needed to expand it to 50 feet.

"So everything in the Batcave generated out from the Batmobile platform. This time, I felt that putting an armored metal motif inside the Batcave would be exciting, especially since Batman, Robin and Batgirl are seen in their armored suits later in the film. The arches in the cave now look manufactured from metal, with a Bat-wing motif featuring the same black/blue color as the Batsuit. And since Robin has now become a full-fledged member of the team, both he and Batman have their own costume and weaponry vaults, with their respective emblems above the entranceways.

"In addition to the Batmobile and Redbird platform, another locus of the Batcave is a large black Batman emblem that slides apart, revealing a six-foot Bat Monitor behind Batman's computer console. Alfred's crime lab still features a combination of high- and low-tech equipment, almost all of it purely fanciful rather than realistically functional."

Discussing the challenges of building the Batcave in the Long Beach Seaport Dome, construction supervisor Greg Callas adds: "It took a huge amount of steel and pipe superstructure to accommodate the set. We didn't have any means of supporting the construction from above, so all the integrity had to be put in from the ground up. We used thousands and thousands of sheets of plywood cut into ribs and cleats, which are then shot with plaster. The set rises 50 feet from the floor, and I had 100 guys working on it for four months. There's a lot of pride of workmanship that went into the building of this Batcave."

The conceptual illustration of the Botanical Garden entrance (left) makes an interesting contrast to the final version (below).

ROOFTOP BOTANICAL GARDEN

"There were so many great sources of research for this set, and trying to create this cast-iron and glass building sitting on top of a building in the middle of Gotham was quite a feat," continues Ling. "The set spanned almost the entire length of the combined Stages 12 and 18 at Warner Bros. The party that takes place in the set has a wacky jungle theme, so the entrance is a huge beast mask with drums coming off from either side for dancers to perform upon. We used projections on the outside of the building facing in, so it felt like there were flames engulfing the entire building. Then, after Mr. Freeze crashes the party and begins icing everything, the color scheme of the projections change from flame orange to cool blue."

Clockwise from right: *Conceptual illustration of the Observatory's interior; a model of the domes; the interior and exterior under construction; the miniature-scale Observatory slated for on-camera demolition.*

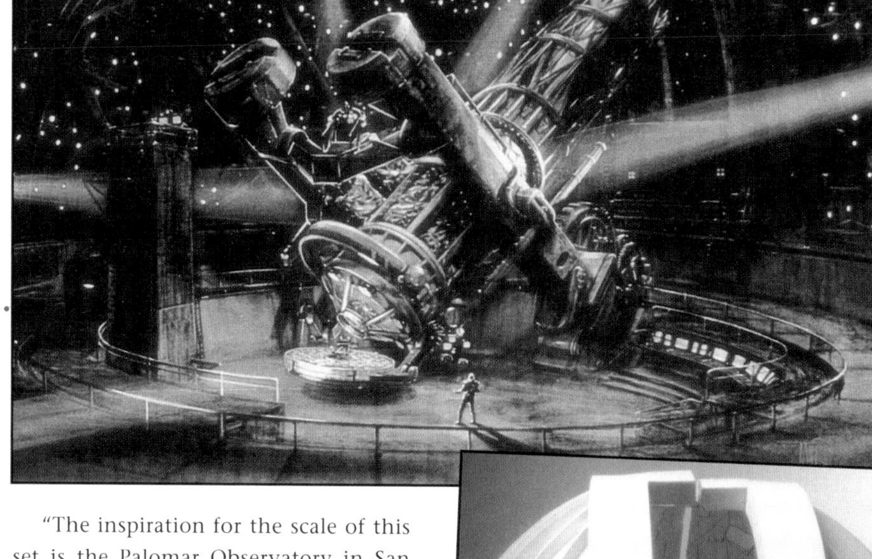

GOTHAM OBSERVATORY

"The inspiration for the scale of this set is the Palomar Observatory in San Diego, which is just unbelievable. The telescopes of today are very modern and almost shaft-like, but in researching early telescopes I noticed that they had wonderful gridwork with a kind of Jules Verne feeling to them. So we fused four different early telescopes into one mammoth, 20,000-pound telescope, which had to be articulated in seven different ways.

"The Observatory, which could only have been built within the even bigger dome in Long Beach because of its size, is 75 feet high, and the telescope itself is 40 feet long. I was immensely helped in the concept by our great illustrator, Tani Kunitake."

Greg Callas adds that "a half Observatory was also constructed in Long Beach to accommodate stunts, so we could get our principal actors in without placing them in a perilous situation 50 feet up in the air."

Right: *Putting the finishing touches on Pamela Isley's tented laboratory.*
Below left: *A production illustration reveals the gloomy Gothic splendor of Dr. Jason Woodrue's lab.*
Below right: *Beakers hold fluids of dubious origin.*

PROJECT GILGAMESH AND PAMELA ISLEY'S TENTED LAB

Batman creator Bob Kane sized up the massive, medieval Project Gilgamesh laboratory, set in an abandoned prison deep in the South American jungle, as "Frankenstein Meets Las Vegas." "Very much so," Ling laughingly agrees. "The crumbling walls, the vines creeping through everything, all try to convey the sense of the world that the mad scientist Jason Woodrue operates in. Pam Isley's tented laboratory is attached to the outside wall of Gilgamesh's lab, so there's a dark little corridor walkway through which she can sneak into Woodrue's side. I used a parachute for her tent and dyed it green so that it had more of a homemade look. This also created a little more of a translucency in her world, against the dark stone of Gilgamesh.

"The equipment in the Gilgamesh lab was based on movies like the original *Frankenstein, Dr. Cyclops*, all sorts of great '30s to '50s movies featuring mad scientists, and then taken one more step by using a laser to cut through from low to high tech. It was a very fun set to both design and work on."

Clockwise from right: *Superb conceptual illustrations of the icy interior and comical exterior of the Snowy Cones factory; the diamond-powered Freezing Engine; a snowman statue is forlornly abandoned in the factory basement; the factory's ice cream making machinery.*

SNOWY CONES FACTORY (MR. FREEZE'S LAIR)

"The interior of Mr. Freeze's lair is in the shape of a cone with a swirl of ice cream on top of it, as you'll see from the exterior of the abandoned Snowy Cones factory which, appropriately enough, serves as the hideout for Freeze and his Icemen. It's all stainless steel with Mylar walls and floors, continuing with the Freeze World motif. Mr. Freeze has brought some of his lab equipment with him to Snowy Cones, as well as his wife, Nora, who's cryogenically frozen in a secret compartment hidden behind a large freezer.

"Believe it or not, the tank that holds Nora Fries was one of the hardest things to design in the film, and went through many variations before its final triangular shape. We also built a Snowy Cones Factory basement on a different Warner Bros. soundstage, which serves as the locale for a big fight between Batman and Robin against Mr. Freeze, with Robin winding up in a giant vat of pistachio ice cream!"

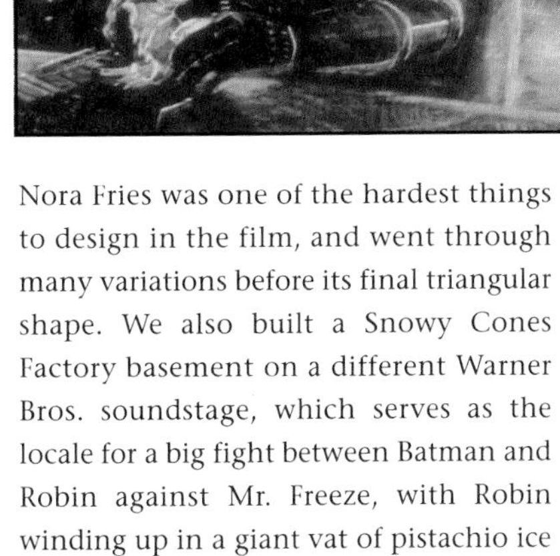

Clockwise from right: *Poison Ivy's dazzling flower bed; a bewitched Robin walks on water; his target, the alluring Ivy; a conceptual illustration of the Turkish Baths once transformed into Poison Ivy's lair.*

BLOSSOM ST TURKISH BATHS (POISON IVY'S LAIR)

"I've always been impressed by European turn-of-the-century bathhouses, which had some very extraordinary and far-out architecture. That was the seed of the idea for Poison Ivy's lair, which is a ruined, abandoned Gotham bathhouse, with Joel adding the Arabian/Turkish element as consistent with Ivy's exoticism. It's art nouveau meets Ali Baba. The ceiling, which consists of holes encased in pods, was inspired by a Moscow subway station.

"The bathhouse is seen in three distinct phases: first as a ruin that serves as home to

the Golums, with Day-Glo graffiti spread everywhere and the central moat dried up; then, as Ivy's magic seeds begin to sprout, creating a rain-forest effect on one side of the baths, while the other is taken over by Mr. Freeze with his requisite ice effects; and finally, in outrageous, over-the-top full growth when Ivy attempts to seduce Robin. The moat is full, there are lily pads so large that Robin can walk on them and huge fan leaves that open magically, which we created from dyed native pampas grass. Ivy has also created a gigantic orchid bed that opens up into a kind of venomous trap for Batman and Robin, operated from outside the set by ten puppeteers with joysticks."

SET DECORATION: FURNISHING GOTHAM

It's a long way from Canton, Mississippi, to Gotham City, spiritually and physically, but that's a haul that set decorator Dorree Cooper had to make when Joel Schumacher invited her to join the *Batman & Robin* company after her superlative work on *A Time To Kill*. For that film, Cooper added realistic texture and visual depth to the sweltering Southern settings. But for *Batman & Robin*, the Mississippi-born set decorator would unleash her wildest imaginings.

Cooper, whose work on *Legends of the Fall* brought her an Academy Award nomination, was definitely up to the task. "We had to have a lot built specifically for the movie," notes Cooper, "but I enjoy that because it's a lot more creative than just going to the store and buying things."

Although Cooper works more than well in the realistic arena, she was also set decorator for such fanciful films as *Honey, I Shrunk the Kids* and its follow-up, *Honey, I Blew Up the Kid*. She says that the Project Gilgamesh laboratory—which she describes as "psycho disco"—was the *Batman & Robin* set she had the most fun with. "We really had a good time strapping the mummy to the chiropractor's chair," says Cooper with a devilish gleam, "and building the operating table on which Antonio Diego is transformed into Bane, adding gadgets to make it even scarier."

Cooper also enjoyed helping to create Freeze World, providing iced-over chairs, tables, television consoles, etc., utilizing clear resin or plastic to resemble the colder but more perishable substance. Working under Cooper's supervision, Dawn Brown designed some of the specialty furniture seen in the film, like the old-fashioned refrigerator in which Mr. Freeze is wheeled into his Arkham Asylum cell. "That was something that we had to have custom-built because of Arnold's size," says Brown.

As for Cooper, every day presented increasing challenges. "This is the biggest film I've ever worked on in terms of the need to have nearly everything built," she confesses. "I have the biggest crew I've ever had, almost the size of an entire art department on a small movie, and every one of them is incredibly talented. And it's great that Barbara Ling has been so involved."

Clockwise from right: *Wayne Manor's imposing hallway; the library under construction, and then completed; the central stairway; Bruce Wayne's study.*

WAYNE MANOR

"For *Batman & Robin*, Wayne Manor has also grown larger in scale than in *Batman Forever*. We warmed it, made alterations, hinting that between movies Alfred was busy doing renovations. There's more use of large-scale paintings hanging on the Manor walls rather than the tapestries seen in the previous film. It's lost a bit of its lonely Xanadu-esque gloom. It feels more lived-in now that Dick Grayson has been there for a while.

"We also see Alfred's quarters for the first time on the Manor's second floor, as well as the guest room in which Barbara Wilson lives. It was fun to give a sense of Alfred's personal history in his room, with leather-bound books and framed photographs of his family surrounding him."

Right: *The miniature version of a Gotham City bridge under construction.*
Below left: *A massive statue in progress at head sculptor Yarek Alfer's workshop.*
Below right: *Two of the thousands of pieces that make up Barbara Ling's Gotham City.*

GOTHAM EXTERIORS

In addition to the above, myriad other sets were designed for the film, including the industrial basement into which Mr. Freeze, Batman and Robin all plunge from high above Gotham, battling in a Freeze-made blizzard, and Dr. Victor Fries's laboratory, described as "high-tech" in the script but actually designed in a style that Ling smilingly defines as "Maxwell Smart Meets *Mission: Impossible*."

Although most of Gotham was constructed inside the Warner Bros. soundstages and the Long Beach Seaport Dome, portions of Los Angeles were also altered to give the fictitious city ever-greater scope. A 300-foot-long bridge—serving as the site for the climax of the film's dazzling motorcycle race—was built in the old Todd Shipyards in San Pedro, beneath the Vincent Thomas Bridge. "It's a very Gothamesque bridge," notes Ling, "with large crosspieces and giant spiked rivet heads protruding out of the centers." The bike race begins in what appear to be ancient Rome-like ruins in a run-down neighborhood of Gotham. "It's the remains of a burnt-out structure with the columns still in rows," says Ling, "that we turned into a graffiti pit with both painted and projected graffiti, which creates a really surreal air."

The Warner Bros. backlot's venerable Hennessy Street, built in the late 1930s and utilized for both *Batman Returns* and *Batman Forever*, was brought into action once again as Gotham's "Soho" district, graced with an intentional pastiche of architectural and design elements. This way-cool neighborhood becomes even more so when Mr. Freeze makes it the target of his giant Freeze Gun from the heights of the Observatory.

So expansive were the film's needs that Ling's work spilled over onto the Universal Studios backlot, where its famed city exterior streets were utilized for the climactic sequence of the new Bat Vehicles rushing to save Gotham City from icy extinction.

But all of the above is, to some degree, just the tip (or the base) of the iceberg...for as gigantic as Barbara Ling's Gotham City sets are, they are taken to even greater heights, depths and width by the spectacular miniatures designed by her and implemented by John Dykstra's visual effects department, with extensions provided by computer-generated imagery.

All combined, it creates a monumental testament to the talents of thousands of personnel in several different departments, all of whom assisted Barbara Ling and Joel Schumacher in scratching that surface of a world of imagination called Gotham City.

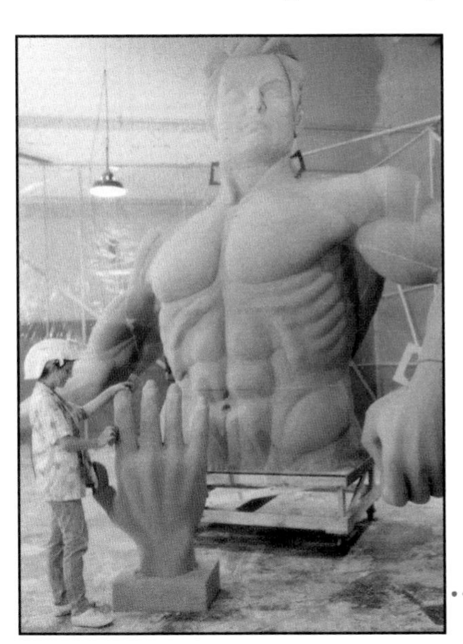

REINVENTING THE WHEELS

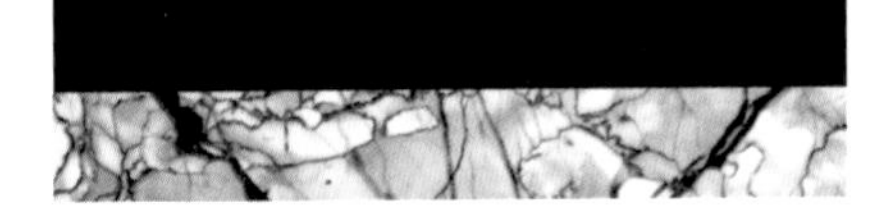

Nowhere is the principle that reinvention rather than retread is crucial to the entire operation of *Batman & Robin* demonstrated more clearly than in Barbara Ling's new designs for the film's dazzling vehicles—whether they're composed for zooming across the snow, through the air, or on good old terra firma.

As she did for *Batman Forever*, Ling worked with a terrific team of illustrators and associates, and the conceptual work would once more become reality through the brilliance of Allen Pike and Charley Zurian's TFX company, whose plain, warehouse-like facility in North Hollywood belies the fact that within its walls wonders never cease.

THE BATMOBILE

If it seemed like Barbara Ling's extraordinary design for the Batmobile in *Batman Forever* was the final word on this trademark vehicle for the Caped Crusader, guess again. The designer couldn't wait to get back to the drawing board in an attempt to heighten the car's beauty and

Right: *A typically brilliant art department illustration of the Batmobile, and a TFX schematic of the vehicle.*

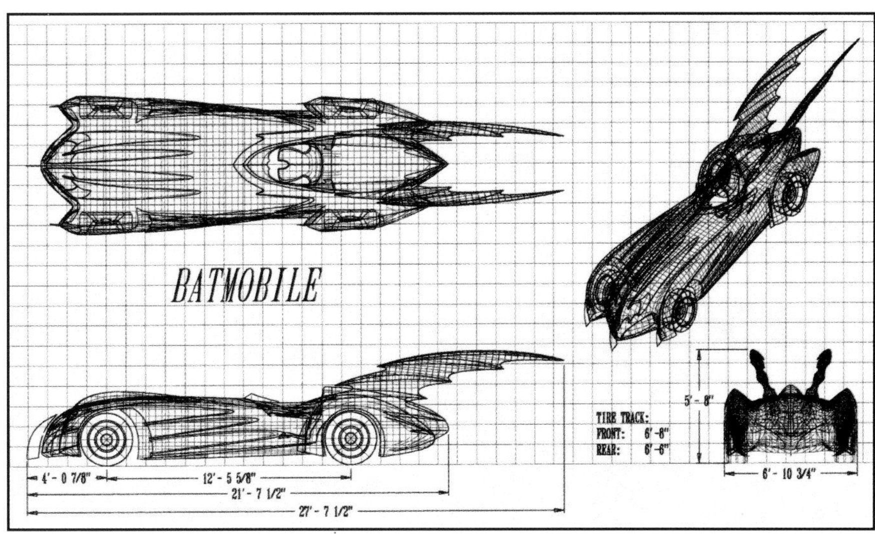

impact. "I was particularly glad to be able to have one more crack at the Batmobile," says Ling. "I think it should always feel like half a block is coming at you when you see it approach, and the size of the vehicle has to take on unnatural proportions for that to really happen.

"Ultimately, I felt like the Batmobile in the last film looked just too small on camera. This time I wanted its shape to be a giant version of some of the early roadster sports cars, like the Jaguar D types or the Delahane 165. I was also influenced by all of the Moon Company's vehicles, including the Moon Spinner and the X Streamliner. I also wanted the Batmobile, this time, to be a convertible, which had always excited me about the early comic-book Batmobile.

"Working again with Allen and Charley at TFX, we did a tremendous amount of development. I also worked with an automotive illustrator named Harald Belker, who once worked for Mercedes-Benz in Germany. The fun of developing the Batmobile was working with the clay models. The central idea in my mind was for the Batmobile's shape to reflect the Bat Cape, and to utilize a tremendous amount of light emanating from within. I wanted the engine to have the feeling of a turbine that was always in motion and projecting light, and it took months and months to figure that out. TFX finally came up with a way of synchronizing the camera to the revolution of an illuminated front-end turbine, so that on film it creates a remarkable animated effect.

"Also, I didn't want just one central flame emanating from one exhaust. I wanted three on each side of the rear—shorter, middle and longer—with six flames shooting out of the Batmobile at the same time. Another change was going to a high-gloss surface on the car's body with a matte undersurface, as opposed to the matte finish of the last Batmobile. There's a single cockpit this time, which increases the roadster effect. I think it's much more handsome for the shots where you have Batman's head right between the winged fenders. The control panel is completely stylized, with animated electroluminescent paper designed by Harald Belker and executed by a German technician."

"It takes a lot of trial and error to develop and build a fully working car that's nearly 29 feet long," adds Allen Pike. "It's got very, very long fenders, blue illuminated hubcaps with the Bat Emblem cut right into the 22-inch prototype tires, which are a special build, and pulsating through the side grated ribs are blue LEDs and alternating yellow and red lights. It's a custom-built chassis, ground-up fabrication, using race car components, including the Chevy 380 engine, which can accelerate the vehicle to about 140 miles per hour. It also has independent rear suspension."

Right: *A production illustration of the Redbird.*
Inset and below: *TFX technicians work on various* Batman & Robin *vehicles in their San Fernando Valley workshop.*

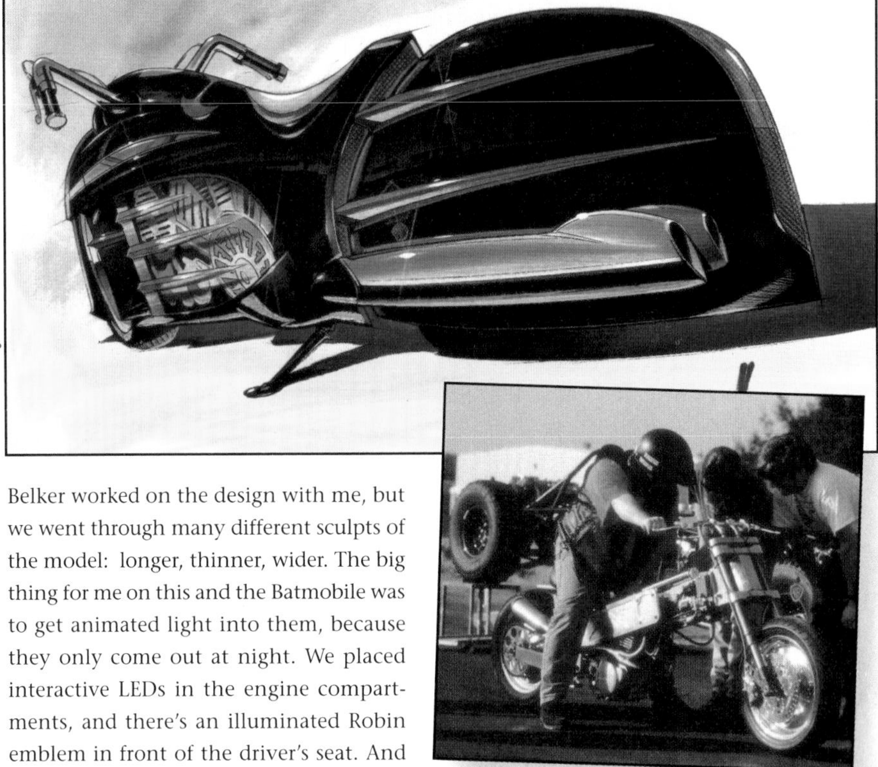

THE REDBIRD

Since Batman now drives alone in his one-man Batmobile, an appropriate vehicle had to be developed for Robin. And since the young hero's skill with motorcycles had already been established in *Batman Forever*, it made perfect sense to Joel Schumacher and Barbara Ling to equip Robin with the world's hottest, coolest bike...the Redbird.

"The Redbird went through a dozen different designs," admits Ling. "When you're creating a new vehicle, it's difficult to figure out how the shaping and the function equal out. Like the Batmobile, I wanted the Redbird to be very, very long. Again, Harald Belker worked on the design with me, but we went through many different sculpts of the model: longer, thinner, wider. The big thing for me on this and the Batmobile was to get animated light into them, because they only come out at night. We placed interactive LEDs in the engine compartments, and there's an illuminated Robin emblem in front of the driver's seat. And again, there's an animated console achieved with electroluminescent paper, which is also utilized for the wheel wells that display Robin's emblem."

Adds Allen Pike, "There was no existing motorcycle that we could base the Redbird upon. In talking with Barbara Ling and the stunt players, we elected to go with a Rotax motor, which is a single cylinder and 605cc, four valves per head, which is used for track and off-road racing. It only weighs about 98 pounds and delivers about 65 horsepower, which is a really good ratio, because the Redbird has to perform some of the most involved stunt work in the film.

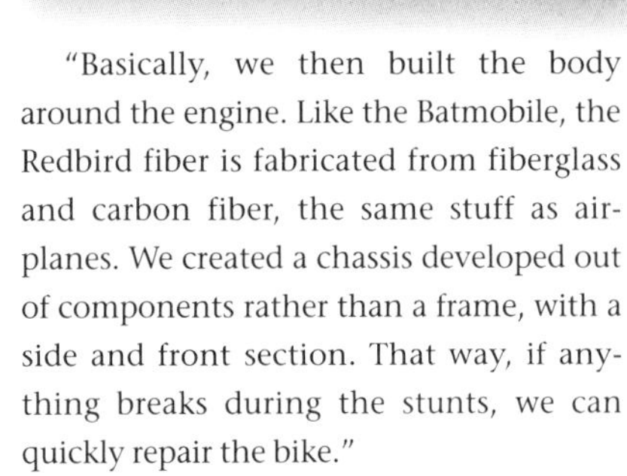

"Basically, we then built the body around the engine. Like the Batmobile, the Redbird fiber is fabricated from fiberglass and carbon fiber, the same stuff as airplanes. We created a chassis developed out of components rather than a frame, with a side and front section. That way, if anything breaks during the stunts, we can quickly repair the bike."

For the Redbird, TFX built one "hero" vehicle, one stunt vehicle that was primarily used for jumping and wheelie sequences, and then two "slider" bikes that were used for sliding stunts and wire rigging.

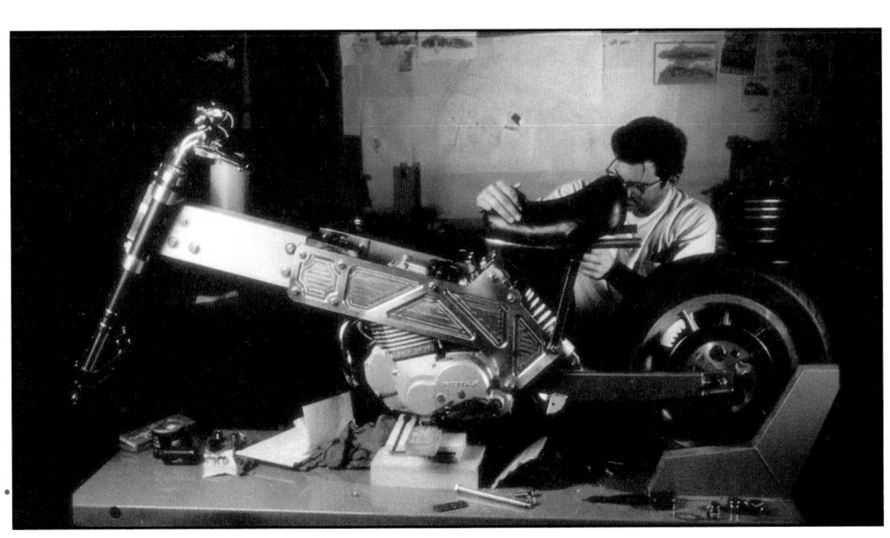

Clockwise: *Various vehicle illustrations, including the Batmobile's revolving turbine; plus the interior of the Wayne Manor Garage.*

THE BATHAMMER, BATSLED AND BATBLADE

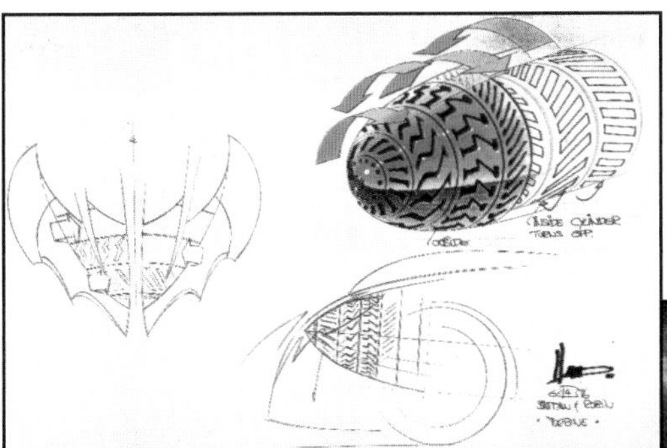

Three all-new, gleaming chrome-black ice vehicles for Batman, Robin and Batgirl also make their debut in *Batman & Robin*. "The Bathammer is based on the Batmobile, replete with a little turbine and the single wing off the back in contrast to the double wings, and a center pod," Ling informs. "Like the Batmobile, it's a single-seater, very tight, and a double color, black underneath with a silver top outlined in neon." About 20 feet long, the Bathammer is powered like a snowmobile, but can achieve terrific speed, and has the ability to fire rockets when necessary. It also maintains a special system to deflect the Freeze Ray.

"The Batsled is based on a combination of a hovercraft and a fan-driven Everglades vehicle, a double-seater that's really powerful. It's equipped with ice torpedoes that zoom along the ground toward their target. And Batgirl's Batblade is a low-slung, almost roadster bike with duel fins coming off the back sides, with ice-spiked tires and a huge, flat back tire that rides very low to the ground. Again, it's dual-colored, black underneath with chrome wings and top."

Allen Pike adds that, like the Redbird, the Batblade is also powered by a lightweight and durable Rotax motor.

Once again, the heroes of Gotham City have a ticket to ride...and take the audience along with them!

SO WHAT'S IN THE GARAGE?

Here are the contents of the mammoth Wayne Manor garage:

Automobiles
1958 Jaguar D Type
1955 Gullwing
1963 Cobra
1950 Jaguar XK2120
1962 Bentley
1973 Ferrari 365 GTC
1957 Porsche Speedster

Motorcycles
Honda Valkyrie
1949 Vincent
1946 Indian
1947 Indian
1969 Harley-Davidson Hydra Glide
1964 Harley-Davidson Chopper
"Schumacher 9000X" (Dick Grayson's customized motorcycle)
"Silverstone 2001X" (Barbara Wilson's customized motorcycle)

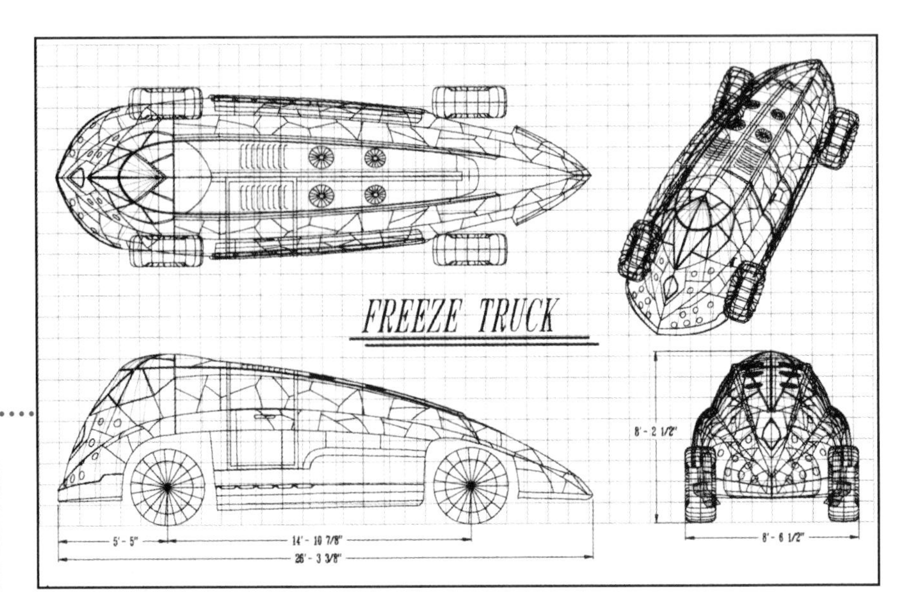

THE FREEZEMOBILE

"This is the big one," Barbara Ling says enthusiastically about her monumental creation. "I loved the idea that for Mr. Freeze's vehicle, you have to have something bigger than he is. And when he's in costume, Mr. Freeze is humongous. We articulated the Freezemobile on the TFX computer, because I wasn't sure if it was going to work. Rather than sit and wait for it to be illustrated, first we designed it in the computer to see if it would work, and it did, beautifully.

"The bigger challenge was that the design of the exterior had to reflect Freeze World, with a riveted-armor paneled front and a sliding canopy top and then a full door that opens to the cockpit. It also required huge wheels, so that it felt like a tractor or steam engine was coming right at you."

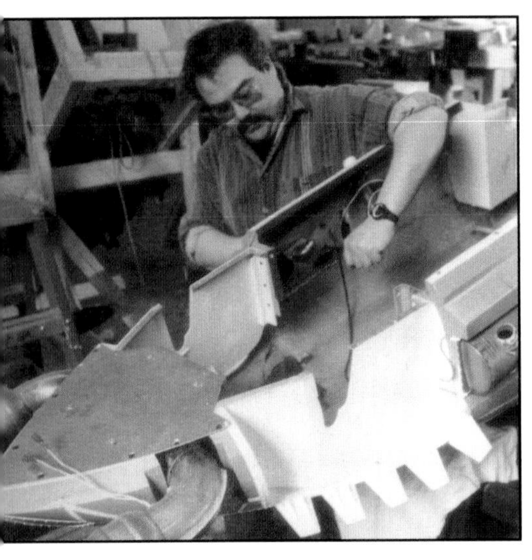

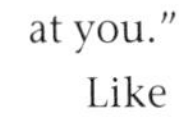

Like the Batmobile and Redbird, the Freezemobile was a ground-up build for TFX. "It was a custom fabrication," notes Pike, "a technique whereby we don't create a clay model like we do for most vehicles. It's a technique that Charley Zurian and I learned from our automotive experience. So the Freezemobile existed only as a computer model in our Alias computer, from which we built a scale model. We refined it, digitized the data, put it back in the computer, refined it again, and then we began cutting the vehicle in full size."

"The Freezemobile is 26 feet long and nine feet high," says Zurian, "as big as a motor home. We attached plywood and foam to the frame, and from that, we used our three-axis mill and cut out the surface of the vehicle. Then we fiberglassed the whole thing, much like a surfboard fabrication technique. Atop of that, we applied foil to give it the natural metal look, along with the rivets, which gave it a very realistically metallic appearance."

Remarkably, the Freezemobile has something in common with a brand-new General Motors car called the EV1, which debuted during the filming of *Batman & Robin*: they're both fully electric! (Not so coincidentally, the original concept for the EV1 was partially created by Charley Zurian

Left: *The Freezemobile in its full-size glory.*
Below: *One of the two quarter-scale Icemen tanks in the miniatures facility.*

at the General Motors Concept Center before he and Allen Pike formed TFX.) Despite its lack of conventional power, the Freezemobile can travel up to 50 miles per hour. "It depends on how we gear it," says Pike. "It has a two-speed gearbox, and it does quite well considering that it's really just an enormous golf cart."

Zurian adds, "One of the things that motivated us to use electric power is because torque is almost instantaneous. We knew that the Freezemobile was going to be utilized a great deal on soundstages where there isn't a lot of room to get up speed. And because of its size, we knew that there was no way a gas-powered vehicle could handle that. In addition, there are so many safety concerns with heat and fuel that we elected to go with the electric motor. The Freezemobile was finally constructed in full-size form in just under nine weeks from start to finish, which even to ourselves was quite amazing considering its size and complexity."

Along with the Freezemobile, Ling also designed the vehicles for Mr. Freeze's henchmen, the Icemen, two squared tank-like versions of the Freezemobile covered with pounded metal and outfitted with machine guns. These were built in quarter-scale miniatures by the visual effects department.

THE FREEZE CAPSULE

This fanciful missile, which emerges from the Freezemobile and blasts off with Batman and Robin imprisoned within, reflects Ling's sense of multi-period design, with the finished product linking Jules Verne's *From the Earth to the Moon* with *2001: A Space Odyssey*. "There were some wonderful old rocket designs that I looked at, including an early NASA missile that resembled the toys you had as a kid, kind of a sausage shape with fins. We added the Mylar Freeze World walls to the interior and a metallic exterior that resembles his suit."

The rocket was also constructed by the miniatures department in a quarter-scale version. "We'll see the capsule revealed in the Freezemobile, and there's a very exciting missile launch through the Gotham Museum skylights," notes VFX supervisor Eric Durst.

THE HOT & THE COOL

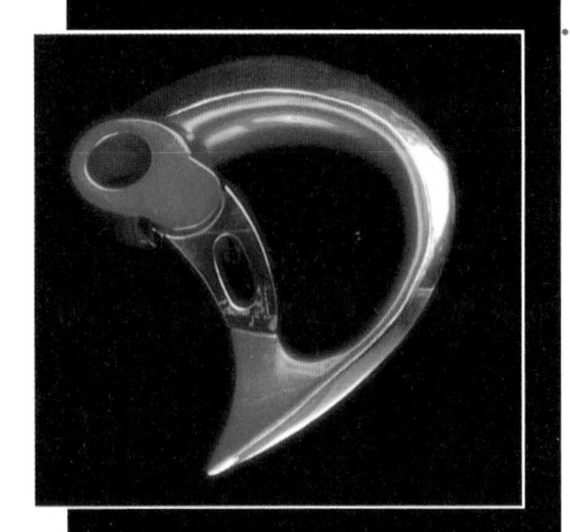

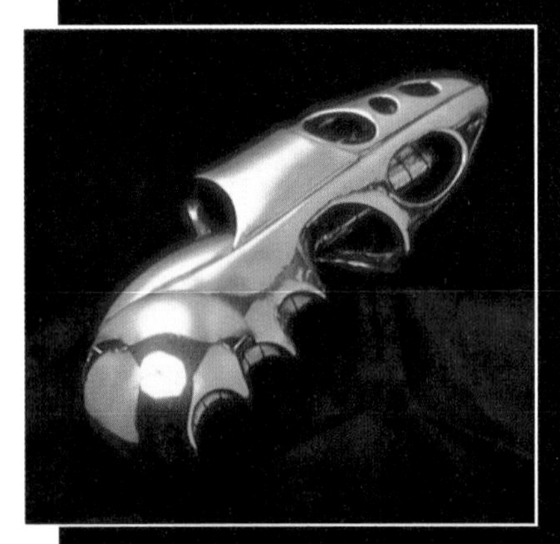

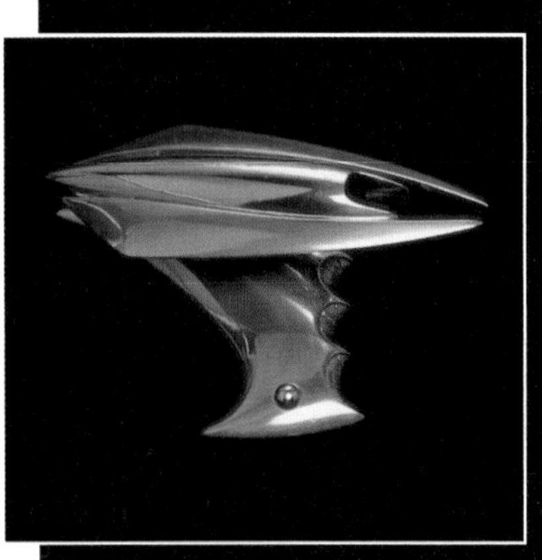

The stunning BatGadgets, gizmos, arsenals and other imaginative props of *Batman & Robin* are a perfect example of interdepartmental synergy. Guiding design spirit Barbara Ling gathered a group of talented artists and technicians: Ron Mendell was the art department's own BatGadget illustrator and model maker, with illustrators Jacques Rey and Wil Madoc Rees also making important contributions; property master Brad Einhorn and assistants Andy Siegel, Randy Eriksen and James Kroning found ingenious ways of creating and maintaining the huge array of items; and special effects coordinator Matt Sweeney and his large crew blazed new paths in making certain that the mechanics were fully functional.

What comes out of Batman's and Robin's vaults was all consistently designed and advanced from the previous film. "The theme was to get more into a full-metal look for Batman's gadgetry," notes Barbara Ling, "and to bring his gadgets into more of a clean line as they develop in each film."

"The sinuous curves of the weapons and gadgets reflect an art nouveau sensibility," notes Ron Mendell, "but the surfaces are like liquid metal. Batman's weapons have moved away from basic black into a polished metal, very fine-tuned and futuristic."

Mendell starts out with simple black-and-white drawings, which Ling reviews. Mendell's more complete illustrative or model versions go to Joel Schumacher for final approval. Then the drawings are handed over to Brad Einhorn and company, who turn them into three-dimensional objects.

Using the example of the powerful, viscerally exciting Freeze Gun, Einhorn explains how such props develop. "It was tricky, because we didn't have Arnold Schwarzenegger personally to figure out what size the gun had to be. The first time we handed one of the mock-ups to Arnold, it looked like he was holding a toothpick. So

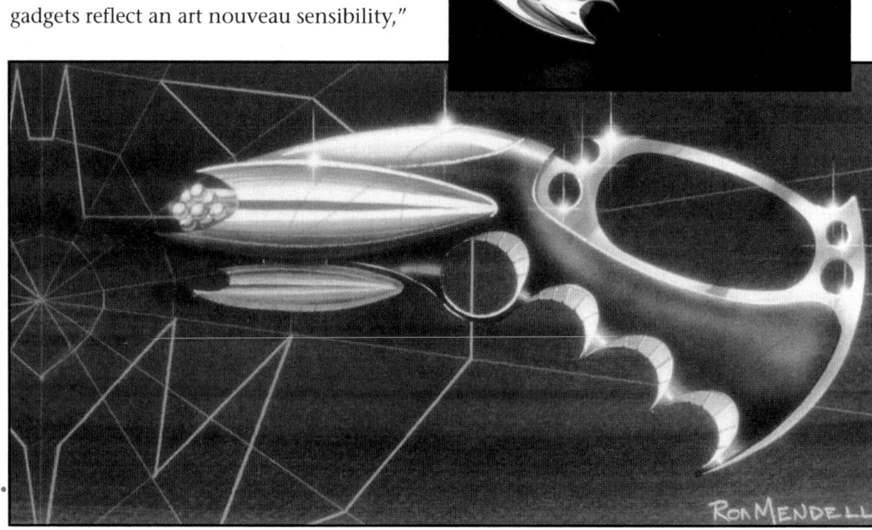

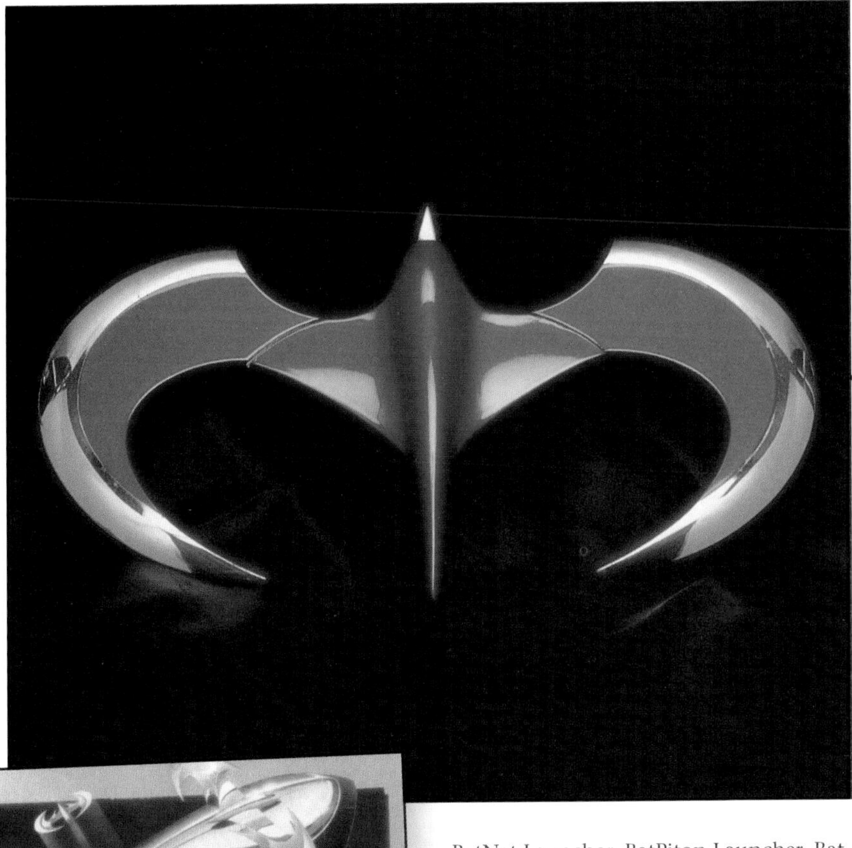

we made the Freeze Gun 30 percent larger.

"Another big challenge was that the Freeze Gun strobes when it's fired, and had to be synchronized to the camera for its full visual effect." Einhorn and Matt Sweeney sat down to devise a solution. Sweeney explains, "When Arnold pulls the trigger, it sets off a complex chain, sending a signal to another unit that's reading the pulses on the camera, which sends a signal back and tells the gun when to flash, which synchronizes to the opening of the camera's shutter. It also sends impulses to the lightning-strike units to flash them at a synchronized time as well."

Mounted in the Batcave vault and ready for Batman to use are such splendidly designed and executed gadgets as the Arm Mounted Bat Tether Launcher, BatLazer, BatNet Launcher, BatPiton Launcher, BatTazer Launcher, BatBomb, Arm Mounted Batarang Launcher, BatIce Saw, BatIce Climbing Tool and four different Batarangs.

Among Robin's awesome armaments are his emblem-shaped Magnets (which he uses to scale the exterior of the Freeze Capsule as it ascends thousands of feet above Gotham), Lazer, Grapple, Throwing Bird and Wrist Mounted Tether. And Batgirl is also suitably outfitted with a specially designed collection of equipment with which to battle Gotham's nefarious criminal element.

Also among the film's incredible array of outrageous arsenals and props are the Icemen's hockey sticks which, true to form, are studded with 50 blue LEDs; Mr. Freeze's dazzling Freezing Engine and icicle-shaped Freeze Bombs; and Poison Ivy's pheromone-based Love Dust, which she conveniently keeps in a Brad Einhorn-designed compact case...just like your mother's makeup case, but a lot more dangerous!

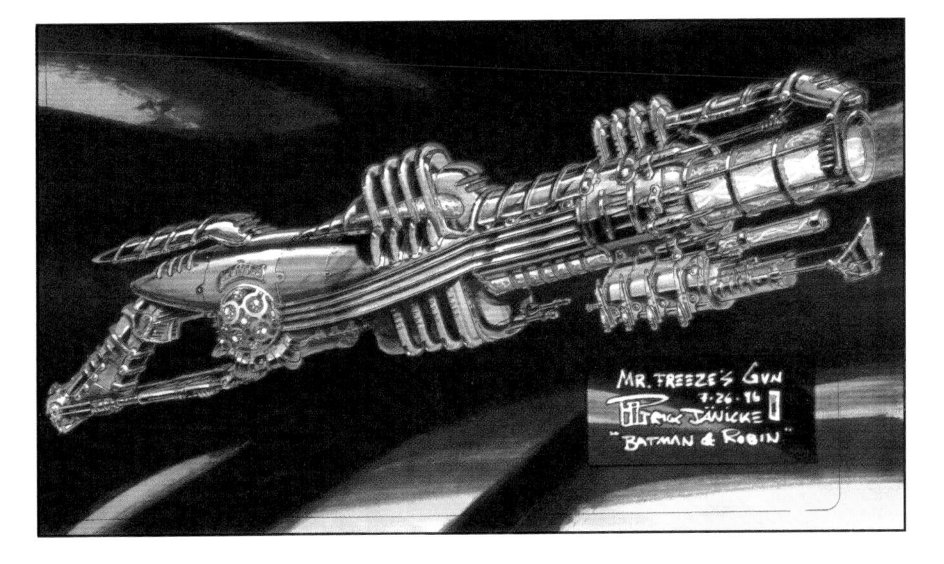

MUSEUM ON ICE

Batman & Robin wastes no time plunging into a major action sequence, as the Dark Knight and his partner-in-crime-fighting zoom into the Gotham Museum of Natural History, where Mr. Freeze and his thugs-on-skates, the Icemen, are in search of a giant diamond on display which can power his dreadful Freezing Engine.

This sequence, only five pages in the script but requiring more than three weeks of both first and second unit filming, comprises a number of action "beats," which called upon the full skills of all involved in their composition. Of paramount importance to such a sequence is the stunt coordinator...or in the case of *Batman & Robin*, the *three* stunt coordinators necessary to pull off

such a stupendous array of twirls, leaps, fights, flights, flips, crashes and mayhem.

At the helm of one of the biggest stunt departments in recent Hollywood history was the legendary Ronnie Rondell, one of the founders of Stunts Unlimited, whose credits have ranged from *McQ* to *Star Trek: First Contact*. Pat E. Johnson, a mighty name in the world of martial arts and a member of the Black Belt Hall of Fame, handled the fight choreography; his credits include all four *Karate Kid* movies. Working with Rondell and Johnson as second unit stunt coordinator was the talented Steve Davison, who had recently completed *The Long Kiss Goodnight* for director Renny Harlin.

"Joel told us, 'Give me the best you've got,'" recalls Rondell in the stunt department's far-from-glamorous on-lot trailer. Thus, every kind of stunt player was required for the film, including those who specialize in martial arts, acrobatics, gymnastics and skating. Called upon for various astounding feats of derring-do were such

major stunt talents as Alex Daniels, a *Batman Forever* veteran who also functions as Rondell's assistant on *Batman & Robin*; Keith Campbell (also from *Batman Forever*); American Karate Hall of Fame member Chris Casamassa (president of Red Dragon Karate's 27 schools in California); Clayton Barber, 1995 U.S. Olympic Athlete of the Year in Tae Kwon Do; and Danial Donai, Brad Martin, Billy Lucas, Clark Tucker, Jennifer Caputo, Dana Hee, Cheryl Wheeler, Rick Blackwell and Christine Bannon-Rodriguez.

As he recalls his preparations for the massive action scene inside the Gotham Museum, Johnson notes that director Joel Schumacher had many ingredients that he wanted. "Number one, he wanted Batman and Robin to display the greatest martial arts skills of anyone in the world. That's the primary reason they called me in. He also wanted much of it to take place on skates.

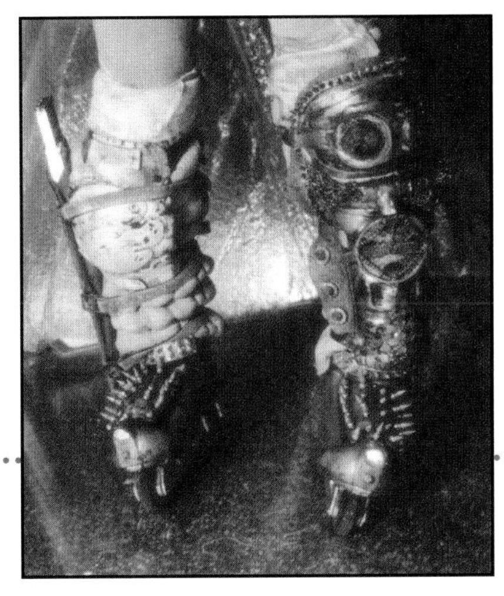

"We wanted guys to skate with power and speed," continues Johnson, "and since we're using roller blades disguised as ice skates, we got roller hockey players for this. Joel wanted to have a lot of extreme skating techniques—flipping, jumping, springing—so we got some of the best extreme skaters in the world. So in any one sequence, which may begin with an extreme skating maneuver, continue into a fight and conclude with a hellacious fall, we might need four separate guys to pretend they're one Iceman."

Working closely with Rondell, Johnson choreographed fight sequences worthy of the finest examples of Hong Kong cinema. "Joel wants the fighting to be intense, but light. So I structured the martial arts so that they're not brutal. They're very athletic, comical in spots and very precise."

Batman's crash through the Gotham Museum skylight and thrill ride down the dino's back, in both storyboards and scene stills, required multiple days of first and second unit filming for a moment lasting seconds on screen.

OPERATION DINO DROP

One element of the Museum action sequence is an extraordinary series of events in which Batman drops through the lofty Museum skylight onto the top of the dinosaur statue's head, and then slides down the length of the brachiosaurus, flips off the tail, and drop-kicks Mr. Freeze on his way down.

Here was a perfect situation for the company to demonstrate the amazing interdepartmental cooperation that must exist in order to pull off such impossible feats.

A week before the big event, special effects supervisor Matt Sweeney explained, "The mandate was for the dinosaur to be both stable enough for the stuntman to stand on its head and to be breakaway. So our foreman, Gary Zink, constructed the framework of the dinosaur; then it was foamed in by construction supervisor Greg Callas's people, and sculpted by head sculptor Yarek Alfer and his crew. We built the dinosaur in big chunks, using half-inch bolts to hold it together. Then we outfitted it with the kind of exploding bolts that they use to separate sections of space rockets, 52 of them to be exact. Before we blow the dino, which is a foamed shell, we'll weaken the structure and cut out the pencil rod framework, and carve away the foam so that when we let off the exploding bolts, the thing'll just collapse into rubble.

"Then we built a track down the center of the dinosaur, with a trolley on it fitted with wakeboard bindings for the stuntman to lock his feet into." He would then more or less surf down the dinosaur's back while attached to a safety cable (which would later be eliminated from the final film via computer).

Before the dinosaur was demolished, however, the skylight and dino-surfing stunt had to be successfully committed to film. "That was an extremely difficult rigging job," Ronnie Rondell recalls after the fact, "and revisions had to be made after we did some tests with Alex Daniels. It had to be reconfigured, because once the stuntman began the surfing descent down the dinosaur's back, it was practically free-wheeling, picking up a lot of speed. But once they got into the corner where the tail begins to curve, that burned off the speed, which we needed to maintain because Batman flies almost 30 feet from the tail to the point where he kicks Mr. Freeze. It was quite a piece of engineering."

In the end, the crash through the skylight and slide down the dino's back was accomplished by two great stuntmen, Alex Daniels and Keith Campbell. "The incredible fitness and skill of the stunt players is just amazing," says second unit director Peter Macdonald. "It went off beautifully, and it just shows how simple the most complex sequences can look in their final version, after so much effort went into them."

As for the actual blowing up of the hapless dinosaur...when asked before the scheduled event by ABC's *PrimeTime Live* what would happen if it didn't go off exactly as planned, the quick-witted (but honest) Macdonald responded, "Well, you'll see a lot of grown men cry."

The following morning, the soundstage was cleared of all personnel for safety's sake, Macdonald gave the order for the switch to be pulled, the 52 explosive bolts did their thing, and the 20-foot-tall brachiosaurus came crashing to the floor just as hoped for.

BEYOND THE CAPE

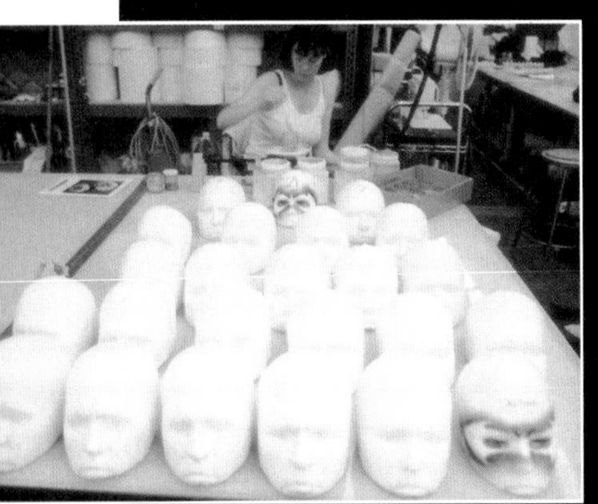

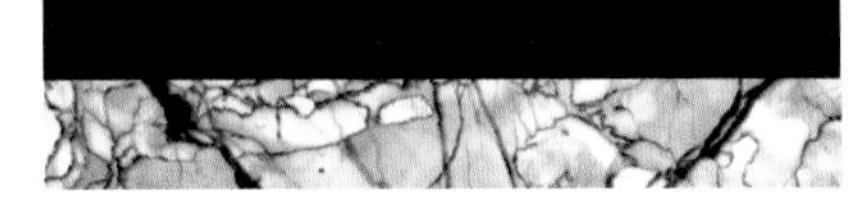

On certain creative fronts, some films require just a little extra effort. Of course, for a film the size and scale of *Batman & Robin*, a little extra *massive* effort is what's called for, and the wardrobe department was certainly no exception.

The costumes of *Batman & Robin* are not just a crucial element of the film's overall visual design (although they most certainly are that). In the matter of Gotham, the fantastical characters, from Batman to the arch-villains, are, in an elemental sense, actually defined by what they wear. Out of the Batsuit, Batman is no longer Batman, but Bruce Wayne. Psychologically, Bruce needs to get into the Batsuit to get into character. Out of the Freeze Suit, Mr. Freeze is...well...a gray puddle. He literally can't exist without it.

So vast were the challenges of creating the thousands of costumes for *Batman & Robin* that two top motion picture designers were summoned by Joel Schumacher and Peter Macgregor-Scott for the task.

Ingrid Ferrin, who collaborated with Bob Ringwood on *Batman Forever* and also worked for Schumacher on the director's *The Client* and *A Time to Kill* (whose realistically sweaty Southern settings are about as far as you can get from the fantasy of Gotham City), as well as the telefilm *2000 Malibu Road*, joined forces with Robert Turturice, a new member of the team with an impressive collection of previous credits that include *Clean and Sober* and the recent action thriller *Turbulence*.

Great contributions were also made by production designer Barbara Ling and, of course, Schumacher, himself a former costume designer with a keen sense of what works and what doesn't.

BATMAN/ BRUCE WAYNE

It's become a tradition in each *Batman* film to transform the basic Batsuit. The newest version is sleeker and more streamlined than the last, even altering the color from basic black to a remarkably subtle but stunningly effective blue-black that's more perceptible in its overall aesthetic effect than is immediately noticeable to the naked eye. The Batsuit no longer features the black Bat Emblem's yellow background on the chest, now going entirely to the fundamental blue/black color, rendering Batman in even darker, more threatening tones.

The *Batman & Robin* team adapted the lessons learned on the previous films to improve upon their already revolutionary work. "There's a continual, ongoing evolution of these suits from the first *Batman*

Left: *The Dynamic Trio in their advanced armored suits.*

Below: *George Clooney in Batman's basic blue/black suit.*

Bottom: *Wardrobe department artists perfect various pieces that make up the Batsuit.*

film," notes supervisor Dan Bronson. "They just never stay the same, particularly in the foam. The new suits weigh only one third of what they did in *Batman Forever*, which was about 35 pounds. There's a lot more flexibility and lightness, but the payoff is that the foams don't last as long. Another issue is that in the past we used black latex, but this time we're actually painting all of the surfaces with the blue element, which has to hold up on a stretchable, movable surface. A lot of detail went into the prototyping and testing of the different paints to see how durable they would be." Different formulas and approaches were also developed for Batman's cape by Claudia Hardy, the Batcape keyperson, and her crew, resulting in greater buoyancy so that it flows more naturally.

And indeed, the basic Batsuit was only the beginning. A second, advanced suit—with powerful, armored highlights on the torso, gauntlets, boots and cowl—was designed by Barbara Ling and sculpted by José Fernandez and Kent Jones for the climactic sequences of *Batman & Robin* (with matching suits for Robin and Batgirl), vaguely resembling the high-tech advanced suit of *Batman Forever* but with even more defined retro-futuristic streamlined details. The difficulty in applying armor to the three advanced "hero suits" was conquered by the magic of people like specialty costume keyperson Linda Booher-Ciaramboli, who worked her team laboriously to find the perfect materials with which to make the armor. Meanwhile, Mike McFarlane of the Batshop developed the perfect silver pigment for the finishing touches.

At least 50 individual Batsuits of both the basic and armored versions were manufactured, many of them suffering much wear and tear during the incredible action scenes performed by George Clooney and

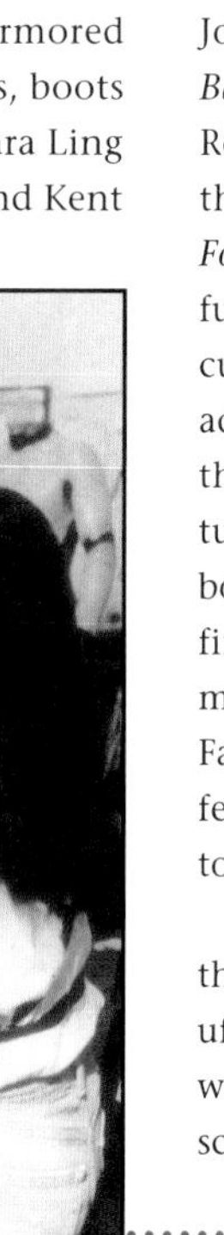

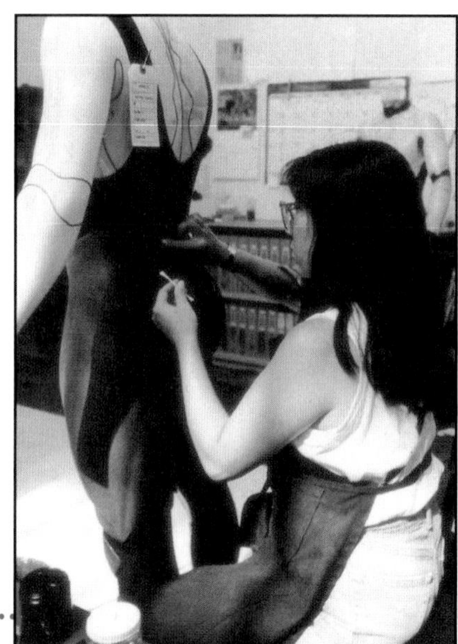

Left to right: *A finely detailed conceptual illustration for the Batsuit; George Clooney comfortably adorned in an Ingrid Ferrin design for Bruce Wayne; George Clooney in full Batsuited glory.*

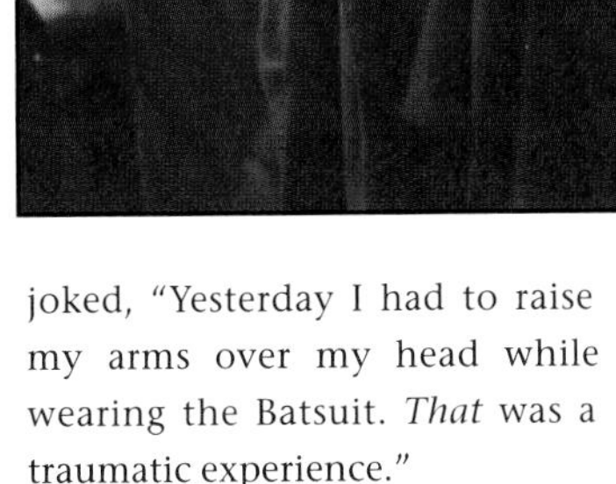

his stunt doubles.

The Batsuit, of course, is created for maximum visual effect rather than comfort, and its unforgiving nonporous latex foam has taken a toll on each of the actors who have dared to don it. George Clooney fought his own personal battle of (or with) the Batsuit with his characteristic sense of humor, amusing cast and crew with an endless stream of quips, one-liners and somewhat more elaborate fantasies, such as this suggestion to the director while shooting Batman's battle royale with Mr. Freeze in the Gotham Observatory: "Joel, I have a great idea for the next *Batman* movie: Bruce Wayne and Dick Grayson wearing boxer shorts in Miami Beach!" Responding to a question posed by a foreign reporter during an international press junket about the most difficult stunts he performed, Clooney joked, "Yesterday I had to raise my arms over my head while wearing the Batsuit. *That* was a traumatic experience."

As for what comes out of billionaire Bruce Wayne's closet, Ingrid Ferrin explains that "Joel really loved the classic clothing I selected for Bruce in *Batman Forever*—turtlenecks, cashmeres, the luxury of a billionaire. He wanted me to once again keep it very simple and black, just defining Bruce Wayne's face so that it never takes away from the character and always creates a great silhouette. So most of Bruce's clothes are black and midnight navy blue, and because George Clooney is so bloody handsome, he wears them extremely well."

Right: *Mr. Freeze (Arnold Schwarzenegger) in pinstriped Arkham Asylum garb.*
Below: *Conceptual sketches of Mr. Freeze's helmet.*

MR. FREEZE

While it's true that the costumes for *Batman & Robin* were a veritable embarrassment of riches, none were richer, more creative, technologically advanced or just totally knock-out awesome as Mr. Freeze's diamond-powered, temperature-controlled (at 50 below zero) human juggernaut of an armored suit and helmet, illuminated from within by cool blue lights that cast an eerie glow not only on the man within, but all those who come near. "There were several hands in the invention of this fabulous creation," says Barbara Ling, "including a wonderful illustrator named Mariano Diaz. The concept of this ingenious costume and its concepts of light were brilliant." Ling, art department illustrators, the techno-magicians at TFX (the company that builds all of *Batman & Robin*'s vehicles) and, of course, Joel Schumacher would all have a hand in completing this amazing piece of artistic technology.

Ironically, this fantastical contraption —with its creatively designed iris-like compartments for diamonds and read-out screens indicating power supply—was actually first fabricated by one schooled in the most ancient art of armoring, the appropriately named Terry English.

Dan Bronson explains: "Four of what we call 'hero suits' for Arnold Schwarzenegger were actually hand-pounded completely out of aluminum by Terry English and his crew, who had come to America from Great Britain for this purpose. The suit, with its 20-odd separate pieces, weighs about 45 pounds. But from those originals, we then had TFX fabricate 15 more composite suits. We took our original aluminum pieces to TFX's head mold maker, Art Thompson, who then took an exact mold in which they shot liquid aluminum zinc oxide, which can withstand incredible heat." The additional suits

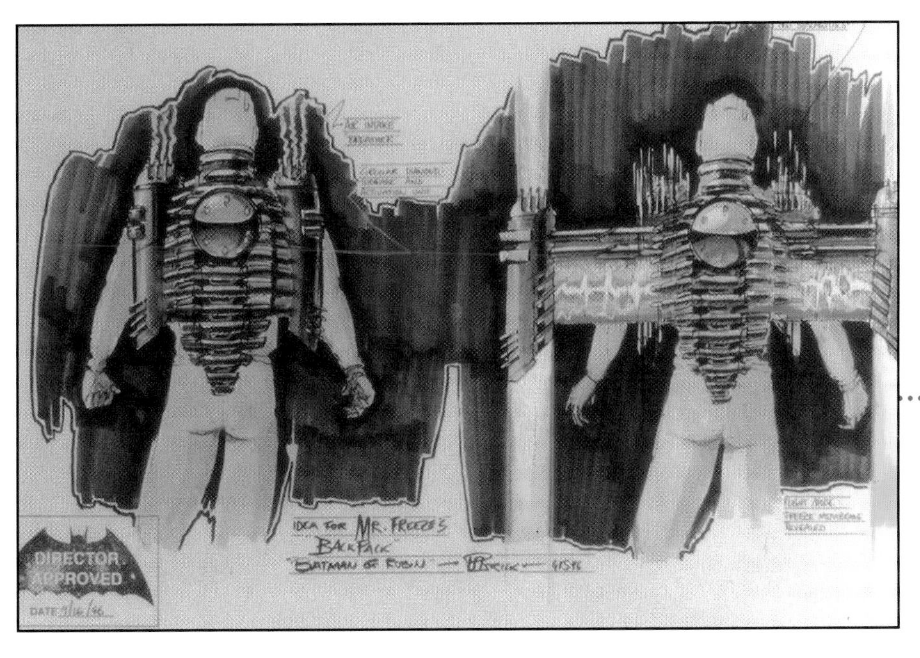

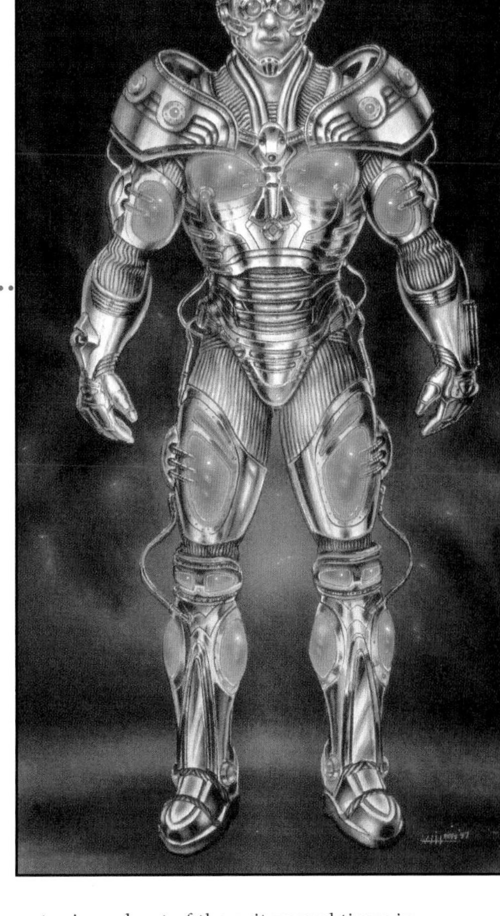

were then created from that old standby, fiberglass, and then metal-sprayed to look exactly like the originals. These composite suits were to prove incredibly sturdy, surviving Mr. Freeze's punishing flips, falls and flights through inner and outer space.

The Freeze Suit's backpack contains the batteries that power the thousands of LEDs placed throughout the suit to cast that distinctive blue light; some of these allowed for 60 minutes of power, while other, lighter ones could keep the suit going for only 10. The profoundly complex electronics of the suit were designed and maintained by TFX, which presented obvious challenges. "I designed the best way to configure the lighting inside so that they could handle the stunts and also be safe for the actor," notes TFX's Art Meier. "The costume department told us what they wanted for the suit, and it was just an electrical problem to fully encompass their needs. Then, once the process was developed, it was just a manufacturing problem to reproduce them for the 15 suits that require 2500 LEDs per suit.

"It's built in subassemblies," continues Meier. "First, we take these thousands of LEDs and string them together, then dip them into a urethane compound, which encapsulates and gives them durability, and then we form them into the necessary shapes for the torso, biceps, thighs and helmet, and run them off a battery pack."

Sounds simple, don't it?

"Well," says the modest Meier, "once the first one was built the rest was all downhill."

Arnold Schwarzenegger presented quite an awesome sight to the cast and crew in his "hero suit," bearing its mighty weight without a sigh of complaint day in and out, maintaining his famed sense of humor. A special chair was created (outfitted, of course, with an ashtray for Schwarzenegger's ever-present stogie) for the actor's comfort between takes, usually surrounded by the five technicians and costumers who literally had to screw, bolt and wire the actor in and out of the suit several times in the course of a shooting day.

Much more cozy for Schwarzenegger—and presumably, Mr. Freeze—was the character's lounging outfit, which he

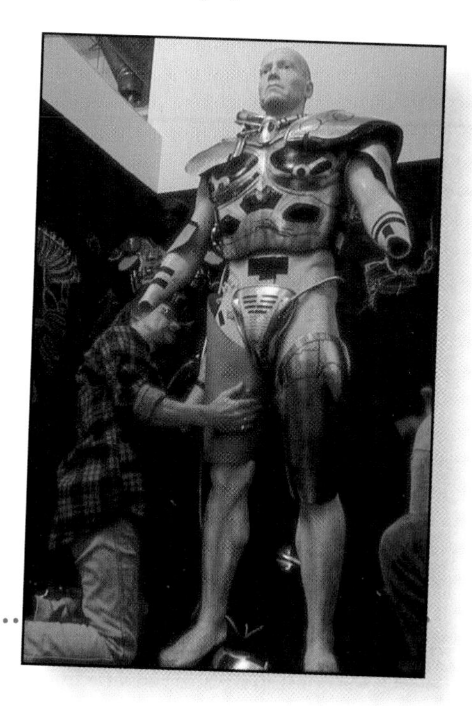

wears within the frozen confines of his Snowy's Ice Cream Cones Factory lair and the Blossom Street Turkish Bath laboratory. Freed from the necessity of wearing the suit, Mr. Freeze's rather elegant taste also reveals designer Robert Turturice's sense of fun, as the mad iceman dons an extraordinary velvet robe festooned with little polar bears, with matching fuzzy polar bear slippers, replete with fangs. "What looks like cut velvet in the pattern of polar bears is actually done with a brilliant chemical process developed by Mathilde Sandberg, the head dyer," explains Turturice. "Next we had to decide on the underlayers, so we used refractive sequin fabric to give it sort of an icy look, and then different linings and the quilted collar. It was quite an interesting, intricate project. All of the polar bears on the robe have tiny microscopic rhinestone eyes, just for a little extra something."

As for those polar bear slippers, Turturice insists that "if you look closely you'll note that they're not predatory polar bears, but polar bears with an *attitude*, which is just right for Mr. Freeze, who has quite an attitude of his own. It was fun to try and create something that would not compete with the Freeze Suit, which is so incredibly magnificent, but complement it instead." Indeed, the polar bear robe complemented the Freeze Suit not just in design, but weight as well. With all the layers of fabric, it winds up weighing more than 40 pounds...almost as much as that stupendous pile of artistically rendered armor usually worn by Schwarzenegger in the film.

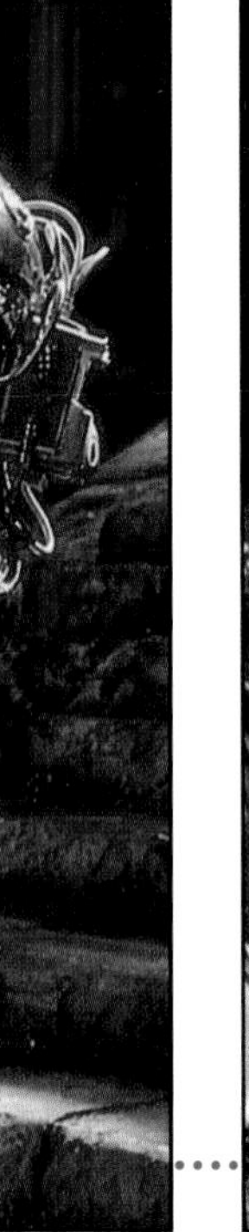

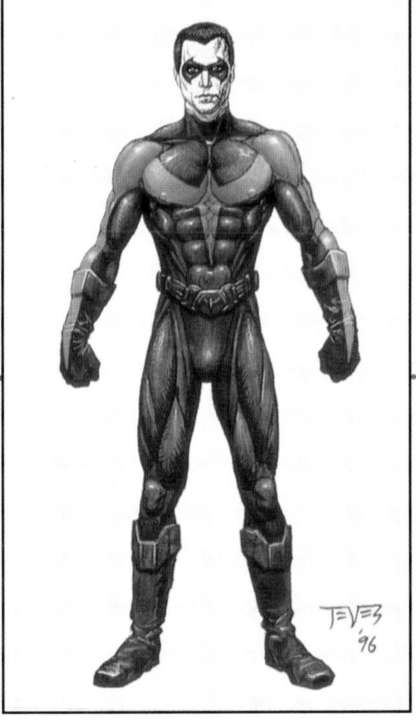

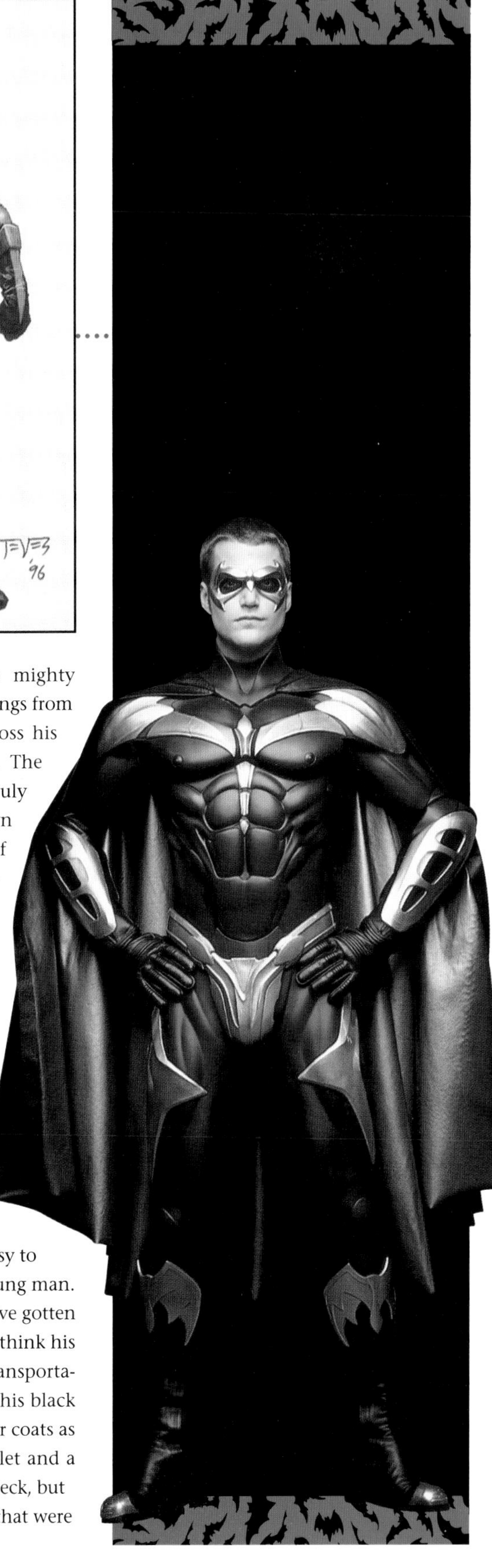

ROBIN/ DICK GRAYSON

Robin's suit has been even more radically redesigned, a further evolution from the two versions introduced in *Batman Forever*: the initial circus acrobat's costume—most closely resembling the traditional suit familiar from the comics, old films and TV series—and the more stylized high-tech version glimpsed later in the film.

Against the striking black/blue background of the new suit, the mighty Nightwing emblem spreads its wings from the center of Robin's chest, across his shoulders and down his arms. The overall effect is that Robin has truly emerged as a super hero in his own right, with only the faintest hint of the orphaned circus boy. His distinctive mask—a latex appliance carefully pasted to Chris O'Donnell's face by makeup artist Leonard Engelman—consistently carries forth the Nightwing logo. Robin also has an advanced armored suit, matching Batman's in its silvered accents.

As for Dick Grayson, Ingrid Ferrin continued her work from *Batman Forever* to further track his progress from circus gypsy to a more urbane and confident young man. "To begin with," says Ferrin, "we've gotten rid of Dick's earring! And I don't think his motorcycle is his only form of transportation anymore, so in addition to his black leather jacket, he's got a few other coats as well. He still has a leather bracelet and a thin piece of leather around his neck, but the other trinkets and *tchotchkes* that were on his jacket have vanished."

Two of the conceptual preproduction sketches of Poison Ivy's costume, and one of the final versions, as seen in the film.

POISON IVY/ DR. PAMELA ISLEY

As sinuous and slinky as a lush jungle vine, Poison Ivy is attired in a splendid series of increasingly outrageous outfits that, as worn by the devastating Uma Thurman, would trap any unsuspecting prey. Poison Ivy's costumes evolve throughout the film, starting with her

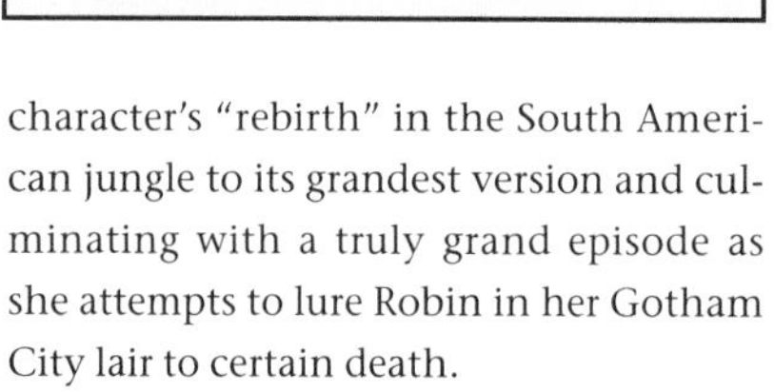

character's "rebirth" in the South American jungle to its grandest version and culminating with a truly grand episode as she attempts to lure Robin in her Gotham City lair to certain death.

The team spent months developing leaf shapes, colors, applications, latexes and paints. Mathilde Sandberg worked tirelessly on the extraordinarily specialized costume department processes of "ombreing" and "devore." Their initial concepts and drawings were the basis for the creation of Poison Ivy's costumes.

It was then up to Robert Turturice to ride herd on the implementation of Poison Ivy's costumes, "and the thing that was always considered optimal," according to the designer, "was that she

would wear latex for what we call her 'day outfit' and her seduction costume. Something that had not been done before was that the latex would be painted, so we had several tests of elasticity and durability. Then we had to consider the actual wearable details, such as a belt that ultimately evolved into a hip belt with a leaf buckle. The leaf motif for Poison Ivy was, of course, essential. For the seduction scene, the neckline of Ivy's suit is scooped out, and these kind of demented, wired leaves are crawling up her chest. And in the beginning of the scene, the suit is covered in spider-lace negligees, veils and sequins, which imparts a mad kind of Arabian Nights feeling. The challenge was, 'Can we get enough sequins on this thing to compete with her outrageous giant flower bed?'"

Quite a contrast was Dr. Pamela Isley, whose frumpy science-dweeb togs were designed by Ingrid Ferrin. "Pamela is a great character, because she starts off bedraggled, sweaty and funky in the jungle, and then morphs into this dazzling creature. But after she goes to Gotham, Poison Ivy also disguises herself as her former *alter ego*, Pamela Isley. So we had to create sensible daytime clothing for Pamela, and Uma brought a lot of ideas to us. We definitely wanted to continue the green motif, even for the Pamela Isley disguise. At the Observatory party it's brown and green tweedy, and underneath there's a very bright lime-green turtleneck and a Japanese-chrysanthemum floral, ruffly blouse over the top of that. It comes off in a great sort of birdwatcher, kooky way."

Right and below: *Conceptual sketches of Batgirl's suit featured a cowl that was ultimately eschewed in the film for a sleek mask and Alicia Silverstone's attractive blonde tresses.*

BATGIRL/ BARBARA WILSON

Also making a remarkable transition—or several of them—is Alicia Silverstone's Barbara Wilson, a seemingly shy schoolgirl who ultimately takes on the identity of Gotham's newest crime fighter, Batgirl. Her attire is consistent with the overall designs of Batman and Robin's basic and armored suits, replete with her very own emblem, distinctive mask and high-heeled black boots, as befits a glamorous young heroine. Once again, specialty costume supervisor Randy Gardell oversaw the newest Bat-hero's costume.

But even before this metamorphosis, Barbara undergoes costume changes that express the contrasting sides of her character. "She's a sweet, blonde thing in a school uniform when we first see her," notes Ingrid Ferrin, "but then we see another side revealed when we discover that she's actually a street-smart motorcycle racer. So at first, Alicia as Barbara appears as this angelic girl in knee socks, but then we see her in leather jeans and motorcycle boots. But Alicia is so beautiful and fair that I never wanted to use dark colors on her all the time, and she doesn't need jewelry to adorn her looks either."

Bane's mammoth personage and imposing character will be familiar to fans of the character from DC Comics, its graphic novels and the animated series, but his attire for *Batman & Robin* was taken several steps further by Barbara Ling.

"It looks incredibly simple," says Turturice, who worked with Ling on the fabrication of several elements, "but it was in fact highly complex." The property department, under supervisor Brad Einhorn, created the practical workings of the hoses pumping Venom into Bane's brain. Even figuring out the logistics of Bane's gigantic boots was difficult, because how do you balance someone of Jeep Swenson's monumental stature and still make it comfortable and easy for him to move around in them? This was a job for Deborah Ambrosino, the remarkable specialty crafts keyperson, and her hard-toiling crew. "Where do you learn things like that?" asks Turturice.

On a *Batman* movie, of course.

Right: *Members of the red-haired motorcycle gang include producer's assistant Lisa Reardon.*
Inset: *Rear-view sketch of dreadlocked Iceman.*
Below: *Doug Hutchison, who portrayed a villainous redneck in Joel Schumacher's* A Time to Kill, *was cast in a cameo as the head Golum.*

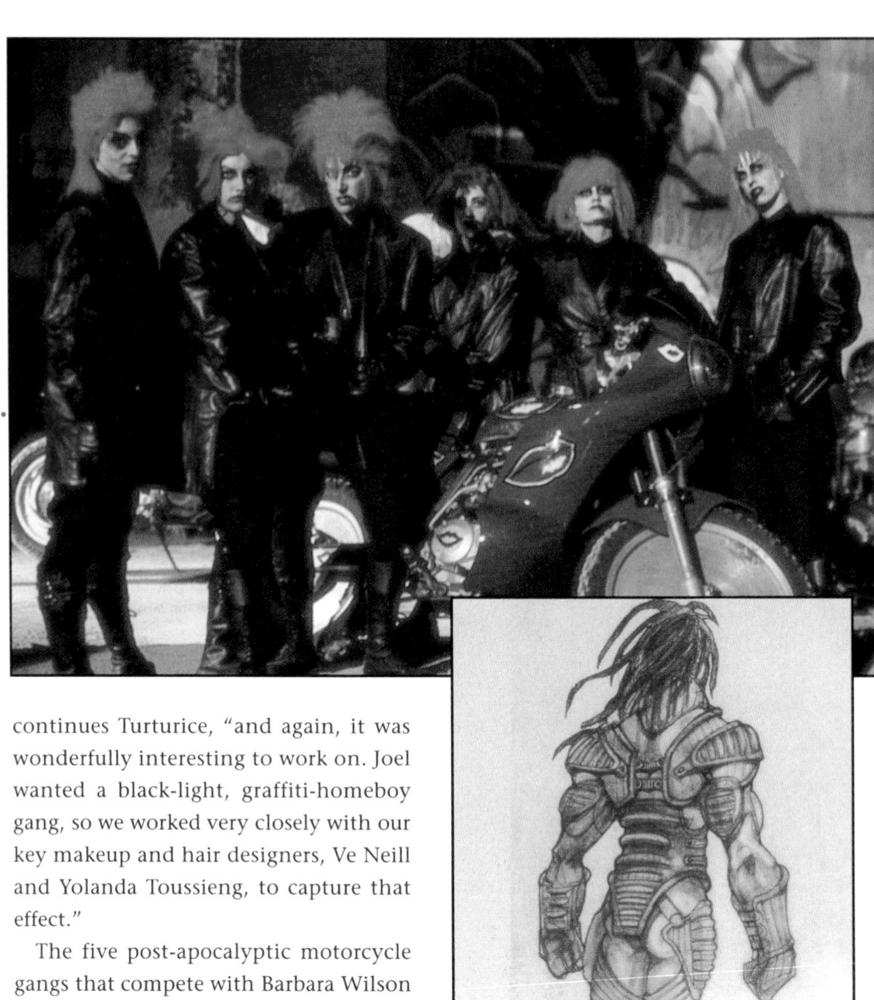

THUGS, MUGS AND GANGS

The wardrobe department, and particularly the specialty crafts and dye shop artists, were unleashed to utilize every spare inch of their considerable imaginations for the hundreds upon hundreds of other costumes required for *Batman & Robin*'s motley but colorful array of thugs, mugs and gangs.

Impressively designed were the Day-Glo outfits for the subterranean Golums, whom Poison Ivy and Bane dispossess from their Turkish Baths hideout. "I collaborated with Barbara Ling on that," continues Turturice, "and again, it was wonderfully interesting to work on. Joel wanted a black-light, graffiti-homeboy gang, so we worked very closely with our key makeup and hair designers, Ve Neill and Yolanda Toussieng, to capture that effect."

The five post-apocalyptic motorcycle gangs that compete with Barbara Wilson and Dick Grayson in the exciting race on and above the streets of the city also presented spectacular opportunities to the costume design team. These wildly creative gangs, designed by both Ferrin and Turturice, included a range of looks, encompassing heavy-metal-kabuki futurism, low-rider grottiness, 18th-century-style punk dandies, a *Clockwork Orange*-esque "droog" homage and a bright red-haired girl gang notable for its inclusion of the usually more genteel and honey-haired Lisa Reardon, producer Peter Macgregor-Scott's erstwhile assistant. "We wanted to make the motorcycle gangs cyberpunk futuristic, but in a comic-book sense," adds Ferrin.

Another astonishing costume featured at the motorcycle race is the coat worn by rap artist Coolio in his cameo as Banker—it's comprised entirely of used athletic shoes! This ultimate satirical commentary on street couture came out of a wild design by British-born head cutter Barbara ("Ba") Higgins.

Mr. Freeze's henchmen, the Icemen—whom Robin aptly refers to as "the hockey team from hell"—both terrify and amuse with their ragtag, dirty-white "uniforms," frosted dreadlocks, threatening face-guards, grinning skull codpieces and ice skates that, consistent with the visual motif of their boss, have small "headlights," which resemble the cool blue that radiates from Mr. Freeze. More than 160 Icemen costumes were created, not only for the first team of thugs, but also for the various stunt players and extreme skaters doing the more dangerous acrobatics.

Right: *The outrageously garbed Vivica A. Fox as Ms. B. Haven.*

Below left: *Uma Thurman disrobes from the magenta gorilla suit at the Botanical Garden charity ball.*

Below right: *Elizabeth Sanders as the demurely attired Gossip Gerty.*

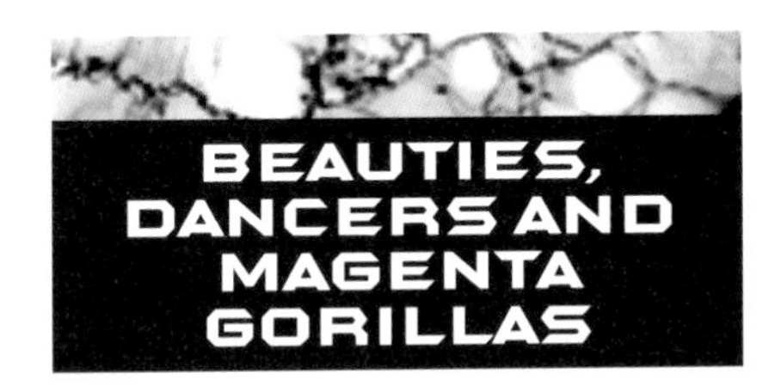

BEAUTIES, DANCERS AND MAGENTA GORILLAS

The costume team also had the opportunity to clothe two of the world's most prominent supermodels, Elle Macpherson, who portrayed Bruce Wayne's statuesque fiancée Julie Madison, and Vendela Thommessen as Nora Fries, Mr. Freeze's wife, who is maintained in a state of suspended animation.

Ms. B. Haven, the gorgeous "snow bunny" portrayed by Vivica A. Fox, is dazzlingly arrayed, a veritable rhapsody in silver, glam glitz and icy follicles. Recalls Ferrin, "Joel originally had it in mind that Ms. B. Haven would resemble a comic-book version of Sonja Henie. But after looking at Barbara Ling's designs for Mr. Freeze's lair in the Snowy Cones Factory, I thought we should do something more futuristic, so I decided to not only use rhinestones and hand-painted fabrics for the snow bunny's costumes, but create a plastic coat and boots as well. Ms. B. Haven also has a clear plastic tail, which is always frosting up, and other Freeze-ian elements, as well as feathers and glitter. We wanted to make it both fun and funky instead of frilly chiffons."

As for Gotham's other denizens, Gossip Gerty (Elizabeth Sanders) "is very comic book," says Ferrin. "She's always dressed to the nines in a sort of very '60s Hollywood style, from leopard dresses to black-and-white checkers to her horn-rimmed glasses."

The charity flower ball held at the rooftop Botanical Garden had Deborah Ambrosino, Mathilde Sandberg and their gangs scurrying to invent some 450 costumes for the assembled Gotham socialites, graffiti stomp dancers and other performers attired like impressionistic animals and gold-plated jungle Jims and Jills.

Turturice is proudest of the magenta gorilla suits that hold a prominent place in this sequence, particularly since Poison Ivy emerges from one of them during a slinky dance she performs for the bewitched Gothamites. But little would anyone know how close the designer had to come to the Yuletide spirit in order to bring his creations to fruition.

Turturice confesses, "The magenta gorillas are made from 450 dyed Santa wigs dipped with black roots and tips," which were thought up and found by research costumer Geoff Lawrence after a long process of trial and error. "We looked at fake fur, at yarn, at everything you could possibly think of, but Joel kept saying, 'I want it very fake looking but also long and shiny.'

"Finally," Turturice continues his astonishing tale, "we got some samples of different Santa wigs. I had a sample dyed magenta, showed it to Joel, and he loved it...and that was the birth of the magenta Santa-wig pelt magenta gorilla!"

Ho ho ho. Just all in a day's work for the *Batman & Robin* costume design team.

PARTY CRASHER

When Mr. Freeze so rudely interrupts the Gotham Charity Flower Ball in the rooftop Botanical Garden by crashing through the entrance in his Freezemobile, what may be hell for the socialites of Gotham was heaven for the stars, stunt coordinators, dancers, choreographer and stunt players of *Batman & Robin*. Another opportunity was presented for them to demonstrate the full range of their talents.

The sequence begins not with flying fists, but with a gloriously extravagant dance that might have made Busby Berkeley sit up and take notice, followed by Poison Ivy's astonishing choreographed entrance into Gotham society.

Poison Ivy (Uma Thurman) makes a sensational Gotham City debut at the Botanical Garden Charity Ball, unzipping from a gorilla suit to reveal her full glory. The outrageous dance sequence that opens the ball was choreographed by Marguerite Derricks **(below right)**, *shown here demonstrating Poison Ivy's movements.*

Schumacher called on the services of choreographer Marguerite Derricks, who has worked on more than 100 music videos and live tours for the likes of Celine Dion and Babyface. During a break in filming, Derricks says that "something like 250 dancers showed up for the audition, which I whittled down to the top 35 dancers in Los Angeles. We ended up hir-

The Charity Ball auction **(opposite left)** *is very rudely interrupted by the stone-crushing entrance of Mr. Freeze (Arnold Schwarzenegger) in his metal-plated Freezemobile* **(opposite below)**.

ing 24 of them for the sequence. They're really excited to be on this job, because this is the first *Batman* movie to hire dancers. I started with the choreography of the dancers, and then started to ease the stunt players into the movements.

"After that," Derricks continues, "I began working with Uma, who was wonderful. She's very creative, so we really collaborated on the dance. Uma is very fluid and graceful with her movements."

Stunt coordinator Ronnie Rondell notes, "One of our biggest tasks was flying Mr. Freeze from the floor to the stage, where Poison Ivy is watching the action. We started testing different rigs, which is one thing when you have a guy wearing a pair of

Levis and sweatshirt, and is another matter when he's in almost 50 pounds of Freeze Suit, which doesn't allow the arms the freedom that's needed for balance.

"What really amazed us when it came time to film it was that it worked perfectly the first time. It's a good thing that nobody saw the wrecks that occurred when we were testing it!"

Pat Johnson observes that the challenge of choreographing the wildly athletic fight sequences in the Botanical Garden lay in the fact that "we were in a much more confined space than in the Museum, with almost 450 extras running all over the place. And again, Joel wanted us to keep it very light and comical. There are some very funny moments in this sequence that I'm very proud of, and we were fortunate to have such athletic stars as Arnold Schwarzenegger, George Clooney and Chris O'Donnell to do so many of the stunts themselves."

Johnson is particularly pleased with what he calls "the tray gag," one of the movie's action/comic gems. In the action, Johnson explains, "Batman is attacked by an Iceman, who's about to punch him in

Below, right and bottom right: *Poison Ivy seems to have Gotham in her very hands, thanks to a wonderfully nifty snow-globe—with its illuminated miniature city—devised by property master Brad Einhorn.*

Bottom left: *Batman faces off with an Iceman, as a waitress cowers in the background. Her tray will soon come in handy.*

the face. But Batman very politely takes a tray from a trembling waitress, and holds it up to deflect the thug's punch. The Iceman hurts his hand, Batman smacks him across the head with the tray and then very politely hands it back to the waitress.

"But then it goes one step further to a bigger payoff. The Iceman comes back, thinking he's learned a trick from Batman, and very rudely rips the tray out of the poor waitress's hands. But Batman punches right through the tray and knocks the Iceman out cold."

Putting the icing on the cake were contributions from cinematographer Stephen Goldblatt and George Clooney himself. Goldblatt placed the camera directly in back of the tray, so that we see Batman's fist smash through it and almost into the camera lens, allowing the audience to glimpse Batman through the hole in the tray. And then Clooney improvised a brief but hilarious "Good night" to the Iceman as he drops away out of the camera's view in a stiff-as-a-board pratfall.

"So you had George's talents, Stephen Goldblatt's great idea and my choreography, and it was wonderful to see the way they all went together," says Johnson. "It's typical of this whole movie, which has really been a team effort. Joel is utilizing all the talent available and bringing it all together. It's a wonderful experience."

A COAT OF FROSTING

Forget about preconceptions or misconceptions about the "glamour" of Hollywood. That much vaunted glamour is actually sweaty, dirty work that takes place in weather-beaten, old soundstages or the often uncomfortable locations where films are made. No other moviemaking division is so closely associated with glamour as the makeup and hair departments, but their central workplace is nothing to boast about either. Specially designed trailers, with a few hair salon-style chairs inside, brightly lit to illuminate every hair, crevice and pore on the actors' faces, allow the makeup artists and hair designers to work their magic. The *Batman* epics, which always carry with them a sense of the outlandish and outrageous, are especially inviting to these artists' creativity.

The team assembled for *Batman & Robin* was one of the largest and most talented working in Hollywood, with three Academy Award winners in key positions: makeup designer Ve Neill and hairstylist Yolanda Toussieng both took home the golden statuettes for their extraordinary work on *Mrs. Doubtfire* and on Tim Burton's *Ed Wood.* In addition, Neill won an Academy Award for her work on Burton's *Beetlejuice*, and was nominated for that director's *Edward Scissorhands* and *Batman Returns* as well as Danny DeVito's *Hoffa*.

Jeff Dawn, Arnold Schwarzenegger's very talented makeup designer, is another Academy Award winner to grace the *Batman & Robin* team; he won his Oscar for converting Schwarzenegger into the extremely believable cyborg of *Terminator 2: Judgment Day*.

With their highly capable lieutenants—Ed Henriques in the makeup division, and Barbara Ronci and Lee Ann Brittenham in the hair department—Neill and Toussieng once again proved that what you see is not necessarily what you get.

KEEPING TRACK

As in all the other creative departments, the intricate makeup and hair designs for *Batman & Robin* required experience, experimentation and considerable alteration until all involved were satisfied that everything was in place. Keeping track of it all can be difficult, and in addition to the usual stacks of Polaroids that both trace and indicate the evolution of a particular makeup, Ve Neill was to rely on a computer as well.

"All of the continuity is done in the laptop," notes the strawberry-blonde-tressed Neill in the makeup trailer, "and maintained on a daily basis by my colleague Ed Henriques. Each character is broken down visually, step by step, with photos and full details. Every makeup is logged with a full description of the scene it's intended for."

Not only was this enormously useful for the first unit, but it allowed second unit makeup supervisor Bill Corso to make perfect matches for his group's extensive shooting. The system, which was formulated by video and graphics supervisor Elizabeth (Liz) Radley, is only one of the several innovative digital accomplishments that she was to institute on *Batman & Robin*.

George Clooney's classically rugged and handsome looks make for a perfectly dapper Bruce Wayne.

"I wish I could give you a better story than this," warns Ve Neill, "but George Clooney is actually *au naturel* in *Batman & Robin*. He's a very handsome man with a beautiful complexion and skin tone, so it's more desirable to keep him the way he is than to try and embellish his look. We're very fortunate in the fact that we don't have to do too much to George to make him look really fabulous."

For such a natural guy as Clooney, the fact that his hair styles on *ER* have, on occasion, been grist for the media mill amuses his pal, fellow pickup-basketball-game enthusiast and hairstylist Waldo Sanchez. "George is the least physically self-obsessed star I've ever worked with," says Sanchez, who was challenged by the fact that during the production of *Batman & Robin*, Clooney was essentially bicycling back and forth between the sets of the fantasy epic and reality-based *ER*, which also shoots on the Warner Bros. lot. Some separation had to be made between the physical appearances of Clooney's Dr. Doug Ross and billionaire philanthropist Bruce Wayne, even though the actor was working simultaneously on both for nearly five punishing months.

"Coming off of playing a military character in *The Peacemaker*," notes Sanchez of the DreamWorks SKG feature film that Clooney completed shortly before *Batman & Robin*, "George's hair was so short that we didn't have much of a choice except to put a wig on him, which was out of the question."

Joel Schumacher, Clooney and Sanchez decided to retain the distinguished flecks of gray in the actor's hair, "because we thought that for this *Batman*, Bruce Wayne is somewhat more mature than he'd been in the previous films. George's Bruce Wayne is suave, intelligent and has an edge as well."

Clockwise from right: *Two views of Chris O'Donnell as the dashing Robin; O'Donnell and George Clooney as Dick Grayson and Bruce Wayne at home.*

ROBIN/ DICK GRAYSON

If Chris O'Donnell looks somewhat different than he did in *Batman Forever*, it's for good reason. Not only has the actor's appearance changed as he's grown into his mid-20s, but the approach to Dick's overall look has altered as well since the last film, reflecting the development of his character.

"Dick is a little bit older," says Leonard Engelman, Chris O'Donnell's makeup artist, "and more sophisticated. In *Batman Forever*, Dick was a bit on the circus punk side, with his earring and pointed sideburns. Now he's lost the earring, the 'burns are shorter, and as far as the makeup is concerned, we're trying to make Chris's face look a little more contoured than before."

In actuality, O'Donnell's face *is* more contoured than it was during the filming of the previous *Batman* opus. "Frankly, I think he's gotten even better looking," adds Engelman. "His face has taken on a more chiseled appearance, and he seems to have lost whatever remained of his teenage softness. Even a few years back, when he made *Scent of a Woman*, Chris's face was so much more full and round. Now it's angular, leaner and meaner."

"Dick's hair is somewhat shorter than it was in *Batman Forever*," adds key hairstylist Yolanda Toussieng, "and in that film it was also several shades darker."

Ve Neill notes, "Being a ward of Bruce Wayne, one of the most important people in Gotham society, Dick has the need to be a little more clean-cut at this point." An attempt was made to retain some of Dick's bohemianism by applying a small tattoo on the side of his neck, "but we discovered during Chris's first day of shooting that it just looked like a dirty smudge," laughs Neill. "So it was one day and out. The camera never really picked it up, so we had no matching problems."

The three looks of Alicia Silverstone in the film: Barbara Wilson in her school uniform (below), Barbara in biker gear (bottom right), and Batgirl (right).

BATGIRL/ BARBARA WILSON

The vivacious Alicia Silverstone, as Barbara Wilson and her *alter ego* Batgirl, also enjoyed Ve Neill and Yolanda Toussieng's touch. "Alicia's transformation isn't as radical as Uma's, but she does go from being a demure schoolgirl to a sexy biker chick, to a very sexy Batgirl, beauty mark and all," says Neill.

"We don't do a lot to Alicia's face as Barbara the schoolgirl, but then we begin adding. When Barbara sneaks out at night to race motorcycles, we add some eye makeup, and she starts wearing a little beauty mark and lip-gloss. Then, as Batgirl, we embellish that even further, including the beauty mark."

That beauty mark is Ve Neill's amusing personal tribute to a glamour girl of the past, Anne Francis. "It kind of reminded me of Honey West, although there probably aren't many people who remember who she was," laughs Neill, referring to the 1960s TV detective played by Anne Francis. "She was a favorite of mine as a little girl, and I just thought that a beauty mark was something really cute and sassy for Barbara to have that could set her apart from the rest of the girls."

Ve Neill and Yolanda Toussieng had a field day devising hair and makeup for Poison Ivy (Uma Thurman).

POISON IVY/ DR. PAMELA ISLEY

Along with the extensive designs for Mr. Freeze and Bane, the transformation of Uma Thurman into her role of Dr. Pamela Isley and evil *alter ego* Poison Ivy represents the creative apex of the *Batman & Robin* makeup/hair department.

"Poison Ivy's a handful," says Neill. "She has quite a few different looks in this film, because she starts out as a nerdy scientist in the jungle, and has an extravagant metamorphosis into this paragon of deadly beauty."

Luckily for Neill and Toussieng, Ivy's kaleidoscopic evolution of looks for *Batman & Robin* was mostly shot in sequence, which allowed them to experiment naturally as the story and character progressed. "Ivy's initial appearance is very much like an earth mother, sexy and beautiful with long, luxurious hair and not a lot of makeup to enhance Uma's already gorgeous features. Then, slowly, Ivy becomes increasingly more outrageous in both her behavior and physicality.

"At the Botanical Garden ball, Ivy is very green, bright and floral-like, but her look becomes increasingly darker and more forbidding—with colors like purples, dark pinks, vibrant oranges, black and charcoals."

Poison Ivy's remarkable appearance is accented by her unique eyebrow-enhancer appliances, which also morph as her look progresses. "The first one she wears is green, then going into oranges, reds and golds," notes Neill. "But in her final look, when she attempts her deadly seduction of Robin in Ivy's Turkish Baths lair, the appliance will be replaced by extravagant eye makeup, almost a tattoo effect."

Neill's makeup for Poison Ivy is brilliantly complemented by Yolanda Toussieng's extraordinary wig designs for the character, which presented rigorous challenges even for one of Hollywood's most experienced and talented artists in her field. "We started the tests six weeks before the movie started shooting," comments Toussieng, "and by the time Uma became involved with the

Right: *Jeep Swenson is the man inside of Bane's mask.*
Below: *Uma Thurman as techno-geek Pamela Isley.*

tests we had already made several drastic changes. We went from red hair to gold-orange to magenta to cotton-candy pink, purple and magenta, all working together.

"When Uma came in," continues Toussieng, "she had a lot of great ideas of her own. She personally needed for the character to start a little tame—as Uma put it, 'a little more organic'—so the first time we see Poison Ivy her hair is a subdued red. Then, by stages, we add more pink to the wig, then bright oranges and yellows and finally, very colorful and wild."

Strangely enough, Thurman's Poison Ivy persona was not necessarily Toussieng's greatest challenge in her work with the actress. "Pamela Isley is equally as problematic as Poison Ivy," Toussieng insists, "because she has to look nerdy, and making Uma Thurman look nerdy is not the easiest thing in the world! So we started with a mousy, straight brown wig, and it was very convincing. We darkened it, put it in a bun, and with the addition of the glasses and Ve's makeup — not to mention Uma's acting skills — she portrays a nerd more convincingly than you ever could have imagined."

BANE

Along with Arnold Schwarzenegger's Mr. Freeze, Jeep Swenson's fearsome Bane receives the most complete makeover of any *Batman & Robin* character. "I called Brian Penikas many months before we started shooting," notes Neill, "and asked him to design an airbrush makeup that would make Bane look like he's been infused with Venom, which was very colorful and fun rather than gruesome. 'Just do what you want,' I told Brian.

"Well, he sure did."

Brian Penikas and colleague Rick Stratton embarked upon an airbrush makeup requiring up to three hours a day, painstakingly applied to Swenson's formidable body in a specially built ventilated tent. "We wanted Bane's makeup to be real comic book," continues Neill, "with the colors bright and vibrant so they would show up well against the darker sets."

Standing outside of their tent on the Warner Bros. backlot during a rainy day near the end of production, Penikas and Stratton took a moment to reflect, rather lightheartedly, on their work. "The entire Bane makeup is done with Fred Blau's great tattoo ink, which we airbrush in many layers over Jeep's body," notes Stratton. "The first makeup tests took five hours to apply," adds Penikas, "but once the wardrobe was incorporated into the design, and Rick came in to help as a partner, we got it down to about two-and-a-half."

Penikas and Stratton paint freehand rather than with stencils, working from memory and full-body mannequins. "We don't usually refer to them," Stratton mock-haughtily sniffs. "But if Brian or I got hit by a truck, then the next guy coming in would know what to go for."

Stratton both knows and respects the Bane of the DC comics, "and it's fun to elaborate on the character and make him the movie's own. The idea was to flush Bane of any healthy-looking skin tone, and then bring out clusters of veins in all the extremities. As if he's about to explode at any moment from the Venom being pumped through his body."

And how did Swenson take it? "Well," says Penikas, "it's extremely cold having your body airbrushed at four in the morning. We can heat the tent, but we can't heat the air coming through the gun." Swenson nonetheless waxes enthusiastic about his makeup artists: "I'd love to take Brian and Rick with me wherever I go."

Clockwise from right: *A Day-Glo face-painted Golum; actor Greg Lauren as the head of the Dandies biker gang; John Glover as Dr. Jason Woodrue; Ms. B. Haven (Vivica A. Fox) makes her move on the disinterested Mr. Freeze (Arnold Schwarzenegger).*

AND A HOST OF OTHERS

There was a veritable cornucopia of other richly visual characters in *Batman & Robin* for Neill and Toussieng's department to play with, including actor John Glover as mad scientist Jason Woodrue. "Ed Henriques did a neat, somebody-who's-never-come-out-of-a-hole makeup for Woodrue," says Neill. Toussieng then added her own humorously bizarre touches, including Woodrue's "wild, ratted-up, knotted hair that hasn't been washed in a while. We put a wig on John and started cutting it to make it all uneven, as if he's been in the jungle for too long and hasn't seen a barber in years."

Another curious challenge was the Icemen, who, according to Toussieng, utilized "a real progression of every type of hairdressing technology that's ever been done in the movies, with a great assist from Tony Gardner and Alterian Studios, a visual effects and special makeup effects house. Holes had to be cut into their masks for the dreadlocks and spiked hair to poke up through, and we experimented with all kinds of products for the icing effect. We ended up using several different types of clear silicone for the Icemen wigs, and then used clear paint over them."

Sixty wigs were created for the Icemen, with 15 different looks. When the masks were removed in front of the camera for the sequences set in Mr. Freeze's Snowy's Ice Cream Factory lair, Neill and her crew arrayed the Icemen with varying degrees of frost, with blue stripes painted across their eyes, "so they don't catch the glare off the ice."

The 300-odd Botanical Garden party guests and wildly attired dancers—stylized animals, golden Tarzan and Jane types, socialites, etc.—required the skills of 35 makeup and hair artists working simultaneously to make sure that every strand and eyelash stayed in place under the hot lights.

Three more examples of the hair and makeup department's range and talent.

Also wonderfully bedecked was Vivica A. Fox as Ms. B. Haven, Mr. Freeze's sexy (and frustrated) snow bunny. "We tried all sorts of new shades of silvers and blues, with lots of rhinestones and glittery stuff, which turned out to be adorable," Neill comments.

As for those two other great beauties contributing their talents to *Batman & Robin*—supermodels Elle Macpherson and Vendela Thommessen—"it was nice," sighs Neill, "to enhance rather than radically alter for a change. Blessedly, their characters were relatively normal for a movie like this!"

Right: *Hairstylist Peter Tothpal slicks Arnold Schwarzenegger's hair down with a water-based resin.*
Below: *Makeup artist Jeff Dawn (left) and assistant Jim Kail (right) apply and seal Schwarzenegger's foam-latex bald cap.*

HOW TO MAKE A FROSTED FREEZE

Jeff Dawn takes a breather in Arnold Schwarzenegger's makeup trailer, surrounded by the usual accoutrements of his craft—scads of brushes and sponges, bottles of colored pastes and fluids, prosthetic applications hanging on the wall like hunting trophies—and explains how he converted the superstar into Mr. Freeze.

Dawn, who has worked with Schwarzenegger on 14 films, starting with 1984's *Terminator*, arrived at the final makeup concept for Mr. Freeze through research, experimentation, determination and guidance from Joel Schumacher. "Joel had this great collage of colors and materials that impressionistically demonstrated his vision of Mr. Freeze," says Dawn. "I began my preproduction experimentation with a double. We colored him various shades of blue, silver, frost-type looks, including little sparkles. Actually, I duplicated some frost looks that I had on *T2* when the T-1000 freezes from the nitrogen and breaks into pieces.

"After four makeup tests, we were ready to do a test on Arnold himself, but we were missing the mark somehow. I thought, 'What happens if we don't go with all these colors? What if we start him off as a silver bullet, and then add colors to that foundation?' That really worked out. I made Arnold silver, and then airbrushed white and blue dots onto that base, going for texture."

A good-natured war was waged between Dawn and Schwarzenegger over the actor's hair. Since Mr. Freeze loses all of his hair due to his cryogenic accident, Dawn would need to apply a bald cap on a daily basis, a painstaking procedure that could be eliminated if the actor would agree to shave his head for the duration of the shoot.

"Had Arnold shaved his head, it would have taken an hour off the makeup process in the morning, and another 20 minutes off at night. I had talked to him several times about the matter during the

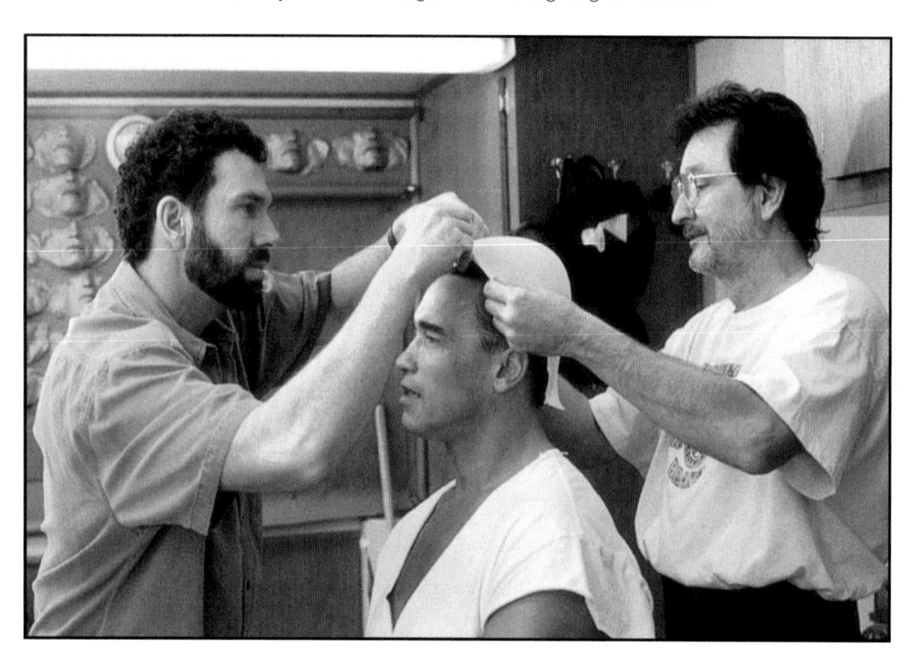

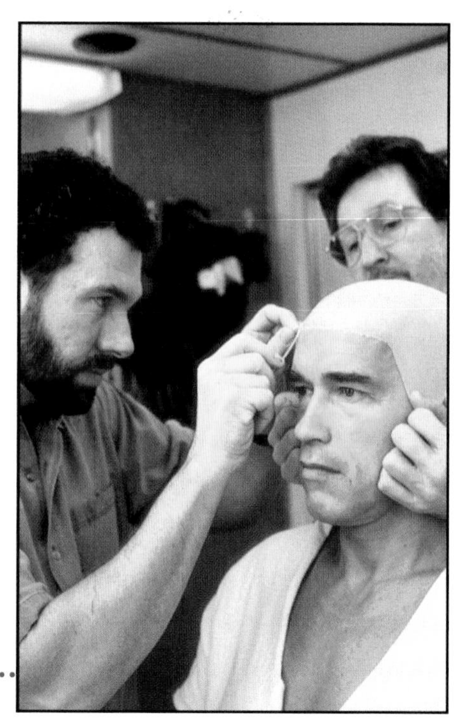

Below: *Jeff Dawn and Jim Kail cover the star's eyebrows with special appliances.*
Below right: *Dawn and Schwarzenegger share a laugh during the silver painting process.*
Bottom: *Applying the finishing touches.*

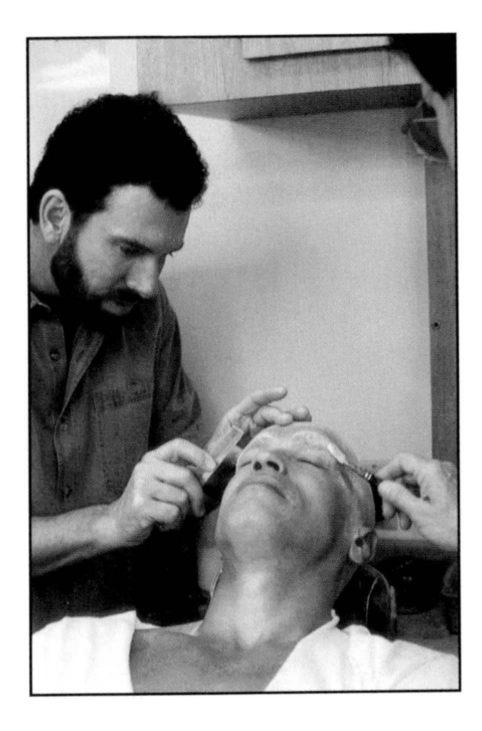

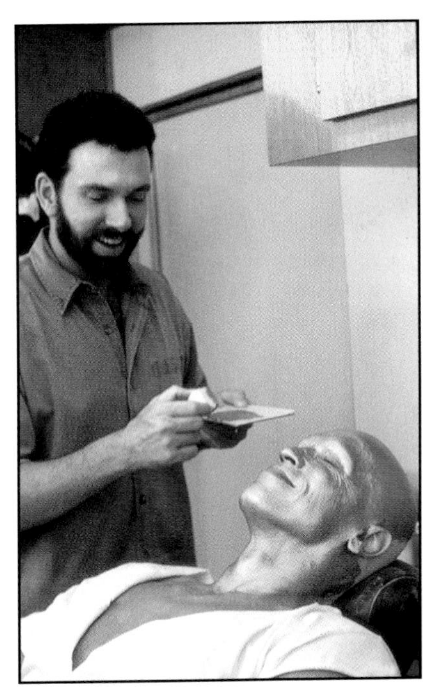

months leading to his start-up date, and he'd say 'Yeah, that sounds good, it sounds practical.' But every time we set a date for the head shaving, Arnold would find some reason to put it off. So we used the bald cap on the final Mr. Freeze make-up test, and then on the first shooting day. At the end of that day, Arnold finally said, 'You know, putting this cap on is really a pain. Let's save time. Bring in the behind-the-scenes video crew tomorrow so they can tape my head getting shaved.'

"Well, the morning came, the video crew was standing by, and I've never seen Arnold like that—he was uncomfortable. Peter Tothpal, Arnold's hairstylist, was standing by, razor in hand. Then Arnold says cheerfully, 'Okay, Jeff, let's put the cap on.' I said, 'But we're gonna shave your head today.' And he replied, 'Oh no, you're not! You touch that razor to my head, and I'll make your life miserable the rest of your life!'

"The truth is," Dawn chuckles, "I'm glad we didn't, because he looks so good with the bald cap. It was a challenge to make it work out well, and it's all the more rewarding in the end."

Which brings us to the heart of the matter. How does one make a frosted Freeze? Jeff Dawn explains the three-hour-long procedure:

"First, Peter Tothpal slicks Arnold's hair down with a thick, water-based resin, which becomes like a piece of plastic when you use a hair dryer. This takes about 30 minutes altogether, and then Jim Kail, my assistant, and I cover Arnold's face with a product that protects the skin against chemicals and glues.

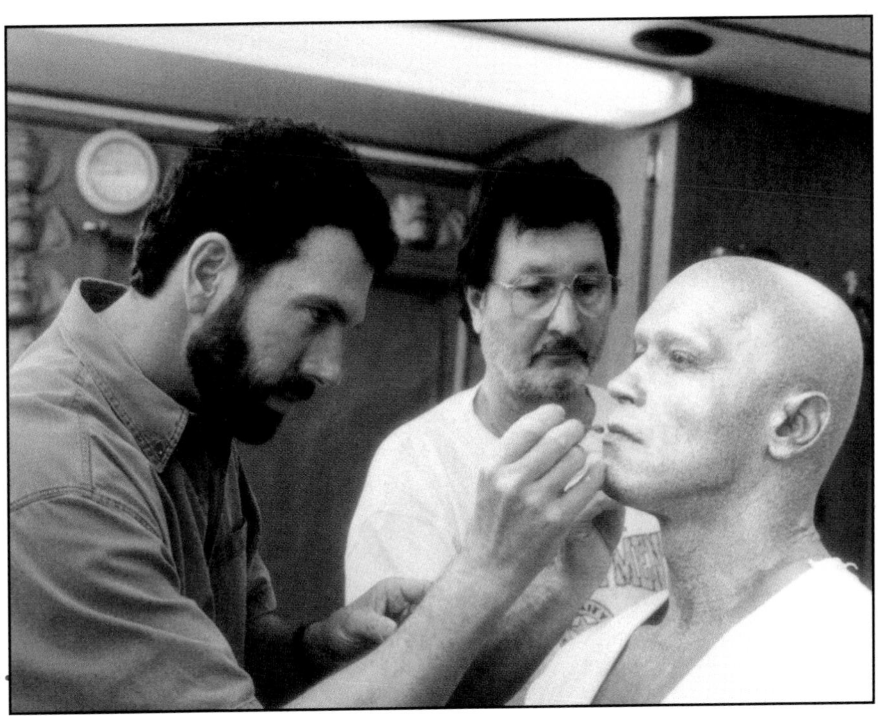

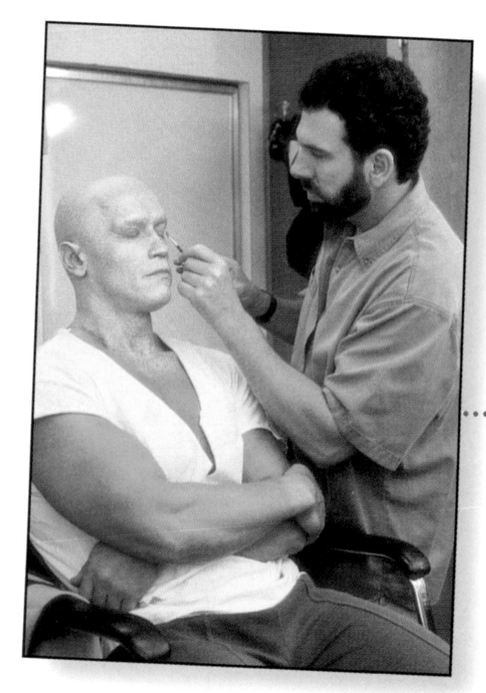

"In lieu of a conventional bald cap, we opted for a foam-latex bald cap, custom made to fit Arnold's hairline and skull shape. Jim positions the appliance, and I glue it down with a prosthetic adhesive. With an appliance like that, you have to be careful because the wrong tension in any direction, and you have terrible wrinkles that you can't cover up. You'd have to take the cap off and start all over again.

"We then stipple a putty-like product over the edge to add more skin texture, so that you can't tell where his real skin leaves off and the bald cap begins. Now we're about an hour and a half into the process, so we lie Arnold back in the chair, and take a medical adhesive to glue his eyebrows flat to his head, and use appliances to cover them up.

"Then to the paint job. We stipple an acrylic silver metallic paint all over him, which is so durable that it's difficult to get off him at night. We paint his eyes and lips and some of the hollows of his face a darker shade of blue. After that, we take Arnold outside to a special tent, and we splatter blue and white acrylic paints to his face for even more texture. Then we bring him back inside and spray him with various sealers to finalize the process.

"Then," concludes Dawn, "we're ready to turn Arnold over to contact lens specialist Laurie Smith, who inserts rigid corneal opalescent lenses that make his eyes glow. Arnold is thereafter seized by the boys in the wardrobe department, who bolt and screw him into the heavy metal Freeze Suit. Finally, he's ready to face the cameras for a 12-hour day!"

They don't call Arnold Schwarzenegger an iron man for nothing!

UP ON THE ROOF

The Mr. Freeze-induced fiasco at the Botanical Garden Flower Ball segues directly into a slam-bang chase across the rooftops of Gotham City. In their respective vehicles—the Batmobile and the Redbird—Batman and Robin trail in hot pursuit of the Freezemobile and two of the Icemen's armored trucks. The highlight of this highly unusual chase scene occurs when the vehicles actually drive into the interior of a giant statue and burst out of the other side, only to discover that a mighty jump has to be made from one building rooftop to another. Batman, fearing for Robin's life and certain that the Redbird can't make the leap, automatically disables the motorcycle's engines, much to his own relief and Robin's frustration.

This brief but remarkably complex

sequence was accomplished through a combination of stunt driving heroics from Ronnie Rondell's team, extensive miniatures and computer-generated imagery from John Dykstra's visual effects crew. Very large pieces of the statue were constructed in San Pedro, near Long Beach, and the *Batman & Robin* company spent a few long nights trying to accomplish the impossible.

"The toughest piece of the scene for us," notes Rondell, "was when Robin is driving down the arm into the hand of the statue, and is forced to lay the Redbird down because Batman has cut off his power. When we saw how long the Redbird was, it was like 'Boy, we haven't even got a prayer of actually doing this.'

unit, the CGI [computer-generated imagery] unit and to ourselves, so that everyone would be in sync.

"In the computer environment, we modeled the 1:24 scale vehicles, remote-

We did get it done exactly as scripted, and the bike was skidded just as described by Rick Blackwell, Robin's motorcycle driving double, but it took several runs, and there were some real close shaves. Fortunately, the statue's hands weren't really a thousand feet up in the air, as they will appear to be in the final version."

That illusion was left up to the visual effects department and miniatures unit, with their astonishingly authentic Gotham cityscapes and rooftops, and 1:24 scale remote-controlled vehicles. "Because a good deal of the chase was to be accomplished by miniatures," says visual effects miniatures production supervisor Kurt Williams, "we needed to have a computerized animatic–an animated storyboard as it were–to distribute to first unit, second

control unit and buildings, so that we could actually decide upon camera placement. Sometimes animatics just give you a flavor of what a sequence is going to be. In this case, we were trying to be very specific about camera angles and lenses, so that we could preview it in the computer and get everyone's approval from the onset. Then we duplicated that in the 'real' world."

Kurt Williams, Eric Durst and Don Baker of the miniatures unit all agree with Ronnie Rondell that the best moment of the sequence is when the vehicles burst into the statue, drive around the hollowed-out interior of its head and neck, and careen down the arm and outside again, high above Gotham City. "One of the neatest things," says Durst, "is that when they emerge from the statue, here's this unending city beneath them, so there's a real sense of vertigo and danger. We've achieved that through multiple scales as well as using CGI and miniature cars."

"The results even surprised us," adds Baker. "We shoot 1:24 scale so much and have become so accustomed to its look, but when our producer, Peter Macgregor-Scott, looked at some of the shots of the vehicles coming down the arm, he was genuinely amazed. It's like a roller-coaster ride. We get so close to our work that it's sometimes hard to feel the true impact of what we do."

SEEING IS BELIEVING

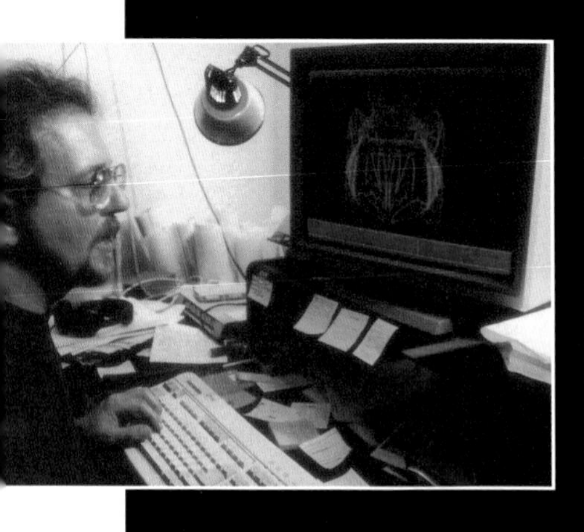

If truth be known, John Dykstra looks and acts like Central Casting's idea of a genius. Tall, bearded, preternaturally energetic, the words pour from him like a bottle of champagne that's just popped its cork, ideas and concepts spilling over one another in a cerebral and visceral frenzy. Dykstra is more than a visual effects supervisor, he's an inventor of new systems and, to a large degree, the father of modern VFX with his groundbreaking work on *Star Wars,* which forever altered the way motion picture audiences perceive "reality" on-screen.

A native of Long Beach, California—a proverbial hop, skip and jump from where much of *Batman Forever* and *Batman & Robin* were filmed—Dykstra broke into motion pictures on Douglas Trumbull's 1973 *Silent Running* before being asked by George Lucas to supervise the visual effects for *Star Wars*. For that film, recently released to renewed audience acclaim, Dykstra won two Academy Awards for his work, one for the invention of his Dykstraflex motion-control camera system.

Dykstra would later become the first head of Lucas's Industrial Light and Magic before starting his own company, Apogee; produce the first five episodes and the feature film version of *Battlestar Galactica*; and earn another Oscar nomination for *Star Trek: The Motion Picture*.

In 1994, Joel Schumacher asked Dykstra to take on the challenges of helping to reinvent the world of the Caped Crusader for *Batman Forever*. But for *Batman & Robin*, Dykstra takes several leaps forward, spinning into the future of visual effects by not only incorporating the full range of available technologies—including computer-generated imagery, miniatures, motion

How to make convincing Poison Ivy love dust.
Top: *BUF Compagnie matches the models—in this case, Batman and Robin—and the camera movement in wire frame on the computer.*
Middle: *Then the animation of the love dust is defined in wire frame using natural-looking procedural animation.*
Bottom: *The image is rendered realistically, with matched lighting composited into the live scene. The result is a seductive pheromone-based love dust that almost has a character of its own.*

capture, stereopsis, green screen — but utilizing them as they've never been used before, for some 450 individual visual effects shots, nearly 150 more than the previous *Batman* film.

Dykstra assembled a first-rate team of experts to assist him in his campaign to advance the art, including supervisors Andrew Adamson, Eric Durst and David Stump, visual effects production supervisors Teresa Cheng and Jennifer Bell, miniature production supervisor Kurt Williams, miniature photography unit supervisor Don Baker, VFX art director James Hegedus —a crucial link between Barbara Ling's and John Dykstra's departments—and an army of technicians, model makers and staff assistants.

In turn, Dykstra and his group called upon the skills of several visual effects houses to handle, under their supervision, important individual elements to be completed: Warner Digital for the Gotham City computer-generated extensions, characters frozen by Mr. Freeze and the rays emanating from the Freeze Gun; France's BUF Compagnie for Poison Ivy's love dust and magically growing plants, as well as the giant telescope Freeze Ray; and Pacific Data Images for computer-generated characters.

The extensive and challenging special mechanical effects—including the swiveling telescope, ascending Batmobile platform and all manner of smoke and mist—were expertly accomplished on-set rather than in computers by Matt Sweeney and his talented group.

At a midpoint in production, Dykstra managed to slow down for a moment to discuss what he was hoping to accomplish with the effects for *Batman & Robin*.

Two views of the Gotham City miniature under construction.

THE DYKSTRA WAY

"Perhaps the biggest difference between *Batman Forever* and *Batman & Robin* is that we've extensively increased our use of computers," explains the effects maestro. "On the last film, they were used primarily as imaging devices, creating portions of Gotham City and enhancements for various scenes. But in addition to that, this time we've integrated the use of conventional workstations, such as Apple computers, to also do our storyboarding, to help design some of the miniatures and to track the development of the script.

"Also, we've moved into an innovative use of the Silicon Graphics workstations (SGI) for this picture. Rather than take the information after it's been designed and decisions have been made, we incorporated the platform into the art department. In fact, we had a computer artist, Lance Hammer, working in Barbara Ling's department with an SGI platform. He worked with Barbara in designing the buildings which make up Gotham. We had mathematical models of the buildings in the computers, and we took those models and fleshed them out in the computers so we had a representation of the buildings' size, scale and position. Then we built the three-dimensional models from those plans.

"So now we've got a mathematical model of the city in the computer, the physical model of the city on our stage, and then we create the third element, which is the computer-generated image of the city. In the last film, we defined

Left: *A craftsman applies artistic touches to a Gotham miniature.*

Below: *The original photography of the miniature Gotham City, approximately 30 feet tall (700 feet at human scale) is taken into the computer at Warner Digital.*

Bottom: *The camera move from the motion control device is taken into the computer so that the CGI models can be animated and lit to match the miniatures, extending them into 3000-foot-tall buildings.*

Gotham as a very tall environment, and we've taken another step in this film. The buildings in Gotham are two to three times as tall as the tallest skyscrapers in New York. And in order to do that, we would have had to create miniatures that were 90 feet tall. Well, we could have done that, but it would be impractical and difficult to light and shoot."

MAGNIFICENT MINIATURES

"What we decided to do is to build miniature buildings that are about 30 feet tall, and extend them by using computer-generated imagery," continues Dykstra. "Because we designed the buildings in the computer, and because the models are built to match, when we extend the buildings we can use the mathematical models as the foundation for the city extensions. In other words, when we photograph the miniatures that are 30 feet tall and have to extend that distance down or up, we simply take our mathematical model and use that to create the extension"

Production designer Barbara Ling adds, "The great thing on *Batman & Robin* is that all of the designs for Gotham were generated out of the art department, and then visual effects takes them over to manipulate them. We actually started designing the miniatures of Gotham before anything else, knowing that we wanted to get into a

This page, clockwise from right: *Technicians fire up the miniature Batmobile's turbine exhausts, and work on various other vehicles, including the miniature Freezemobile.*
Opposite, top: *A computer screen from Warner Digital showing the controls and renderings for the Freeze Beam animation.*
Bottom: *A live museum guard is reconstructed on the computers at Warner Digital and shrouded in computer-generated ice.*

larger spectrum of miniatures and begin shooting earlier. So the miniatures were actually built well before any of the main sets.

"This time, the miniatures include trains running on tracks between buildings high above the city, vehicles moving along elevated bridges and highways, rear-projected animated signage, all of the things we wanted to do last time but couldn't, either because of time or technology."

"We made the buildings more Gotham-esque this time," notes Kurt Williams in the nondescript San Fernando Valley facility that incongruously contains a stunning world of wonders. "There are more sculptures, more details, and that's why the build started in February 1996, seven months before the start of principal photography."

Don Baker adds, "'Miniature' may seem a strange word, considering that most of the Gotham buildings are at least 20 or 25 feet tall, and the avenues are so large that we can walk between them and really enjoy the grandeur."

Some 26 miniature buildings, built on 1:24 scale, were constructed for Gotham City, all of them moveable to create different cityscapes for different sequences. A computerized motion-control camera was utilized, according to Baker, "to provide a camera motion that's repeatable, and can travel the same path of action multiple times at multiple camera speeds."

"Also," says Williams, "we have to sometimes match different live-action plates and computer SGI plates, so all the data of the motion-control set-up has to be equated in the computer world as well."

It wasn't just the skyscrapers, bridges and highways of Gotham that Williams, Durst and Baker needed to create, but the dazzling vehicles as well. "In miniature, we're working with the vehicles in two scales," offers Durst, "both 1:24 and quar-

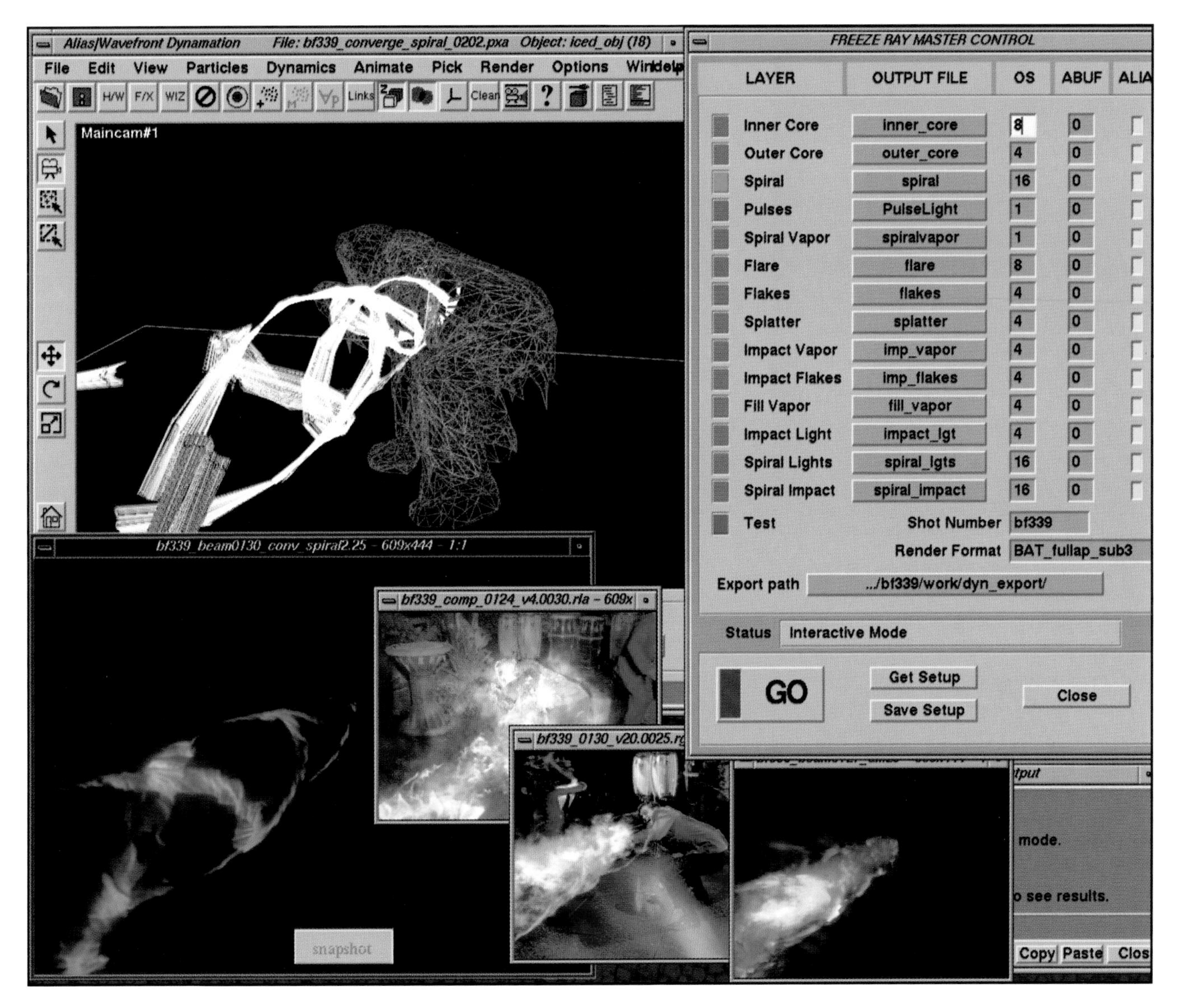

ter-scale. The full-size Batmobile is 29 feet long, and ours is about seven feet long, which is pretty big for a miniature. We also had to match the real Batmobile's intricate lighting system, revolving turbine and six exhaust flames, which was a big challenge. Matching was vital, so every step of the way we've been in communication with the first unit. We've got 15 onboard lighting systems in the miniature Batmobile in order to match the first unit effects for the car. Duplicating in quarter-scale is four times as difficult."

The miniatures department also created a miniature, radio-controlled Freezemobile, armored Icemen tanks and boxy, built-for-function Gotham City passenger cars, all with four-wheel drive, four-wheel braking and independent suspension!

CGG: COMPUTER-GENERATED GENIUS

"We're also using the computer to create our camera moves," Dykstra offers. "Because the computers have become fast enough and the software capable enough for this application, we can create three-dimensional moving images of what a special effects scene is meant to be, and in some cases we've used the same program to help define spaces to determine camera angles for the live-action stuff as well."

For the *Batman & Robin* VFX department, the "real world" spills out from the computer and obversely, elements of reality also

How to ice a clock tower. ***From top:*** *A 1:24 scale miniature clock tower is scanned into digital information at E-Film and sent to BUF Compagnie; a wire-frame model of the computer ice is constructed; the wire-frame model is tracked onto the miniature to match the camera movement.*

go into the computer. Effects supervisor Andrew Adamson elaborates: "This is a technique that we're experimenting with, and have developed considerably for this film, called stereopsis. We're using this quite a bit for the icing of the people and the locating of buildings in Gotham City. One of the methods we use is to place a number of LEDs that blink at a very high frequency. In the scene, we measure those with a type of surveying device called a laser theodolite, so we know their positions in space. Then, when you get even a fast camera move, you get a sharp dot and know the points in the two-dimensional image by using the lens information and the starting position of the camera, you can track the camera for the rest of the move.

"For example, to apply ice to a person who's been hit by the rays of the Freeze Gun, you need a three-dimensional model of the person. So we measure the points, then go in and manually pick points to capture texture information from the reference cameras, then reconstruct the scene, which allows us to apply the ice to the characters and do a technique called 'ray tracing,' where we literally trace every ray of light. You get the most beautiful light refraction, which gives it a real dimensional quality in the finished version. The idea is to get as much a sense of animation as possible, to keep the energy in it. For the Freeze Gun ray, we want something that's kind of a combination of natural organics and almost an electrical field. One of the things that we liked is the feeling that the beam is actually sucking the cold out of the air, so you get this gas that goes into the beam and then is projected out to the character being frozen."

Top: *Surface information and shading is applied to the model to evaluate the shape.*
Middle: *The model is "ray traced" into the miniature scene, also reconstructed digitally, to add the refraction and reflections expected of a real solid object.*
Bottom: *Two frozen bodies beautifully sculpted by Rick Baker's talented team.*

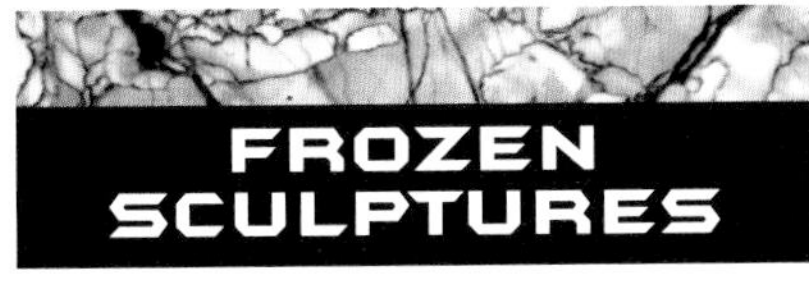

FROZEN SCULPTURES

As an example of how different visual effects divisions work together to achieve an overall effect, frozen ice bodies were also sculpted for use on-set rather than in-computer by Rick Baker, the multiple Oscar-winning special and makeup effects artist, who previously contributed to both *Batman Returns* and *Batman Forever*. "We made six frozen figures," notes Chad Waters, one of Baker's on-set artists, "which we based on body casts of the actor in a director-approved position. From there, we created a fiberglass body. The face casts were cleaned and given expression if it wasn't captured in the original live cast. Then sculptures were made to represent the ice, made of a very clear resin, topped with a coated urethane."

These frozen bodies impressed many as extraordinary works of modern sculptural

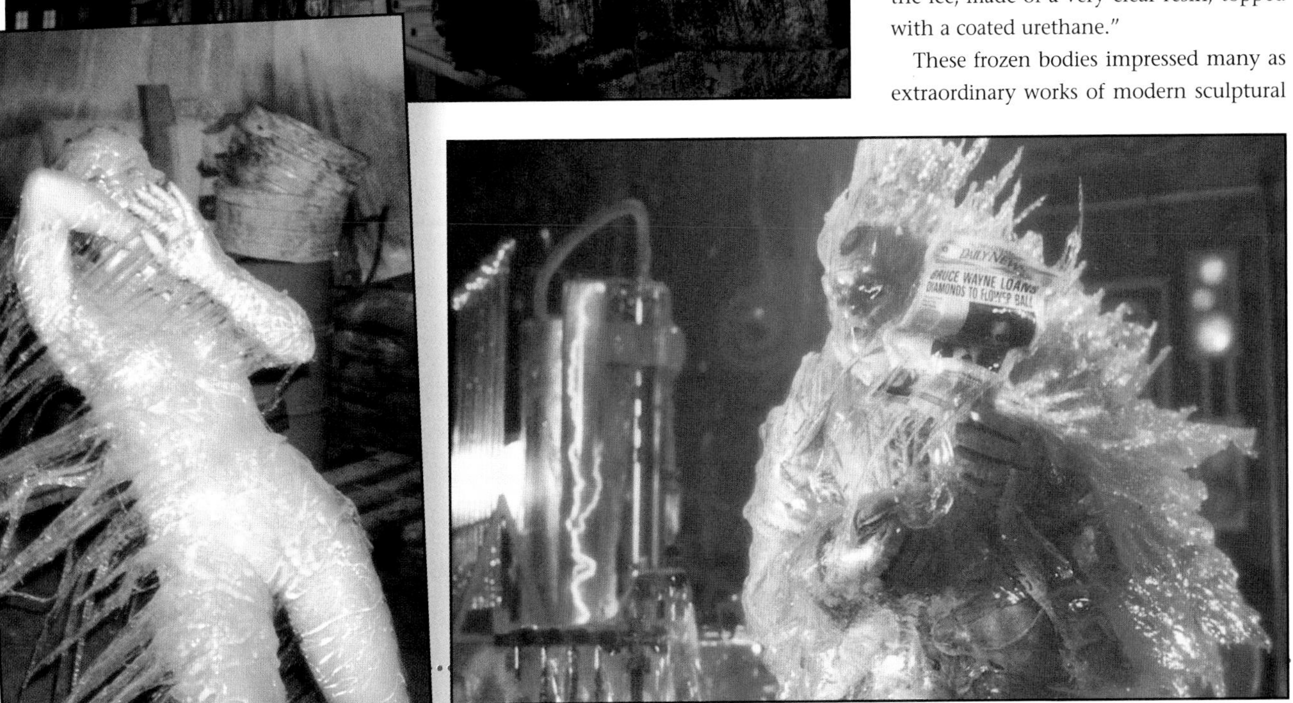

Original storyboards of Robin skyboarding through Gotham after freeing Batman and himself from Mr. Freeze's airborne capsule. These sequences will ultimately be accomplished through a combination of real actors, stunt players and digital characters.

art in themselves, and the fabulous Baker boys also created an astonishingly lifelike Nora Fries—in frozen suspended animation—from silicone and paint, carefully based on Vendela Thommessen's facial and body cast.

DIGITAL STUNTMEN

What happens when a motion picture sequence features a stunt so phenomenally dangerous that even the bravest stunt player alive wouldn't dare put his/her butt on the line (or the smartest director would never allow them to)—such as the one in *Batman & Robin* in which our heroes leap out of an ascending rocket 20,000 feet above Gotham and skyboard to Earth?

The answer is a brand-new one, and *Batman & Robin* is among the first films to attempt it...digital stuntmen!

Explains John Dykstra, "They did it in *Jurassic Park* and we did it in *Batman Forever*. We weren't certain that we could create a three-dimensional Batman figure indistinguishable from the live-action character, but we did. We all went into it with our eyes open, saying, 'This is something we can't do right now, and we're not sure whether the technology will catch up in time to allow us to do it.' But we had to assume that statistically, the rate of advance of capabilities would keep up with our appetite for technology."

Andrew Adamson adds, "Pacific Data Images worked with us on the digital characters on *Batman Forever*, and there's a lot more for them to do this time. Last time, it was relatively simple. We used the characters at a further distance, but this time, we're actually going to have musculature and facial detail."

The visual effects crew began to lay out the sequence in a fairly simple computerized animatic, and then utilized the motion-capture technique to add skin to the bones, so to speak. Explains Adamson, "Motion capture is when you have multiple cameras and infrared sensors laced on the body. By analyzing the data, we get back an image that is basically a whole series of dots, and we can figure out where these dots were in space and then can actually track a motion of the person.

"In this case, we actually set up some motion-capture cameras in a vertical wind tunnel on a military base in North Carolina usually used for skydiving practice. We put a guy in there on a skyboard, and captured his motion, which Pacific Data Images then applied to the digital figures. Thus, we can get all the little nuances of balance and shifting and direction that you see with a real skyboarder. The final sequence will be a combination of digital figures, the real actors and stunt players."

Right: *The live scene of Poison Ivy (Uma Thurman) and Bane (Jeep Swenson) is scanned digitally and then moved onto the computers at BUF Compagnie, tracking the tiny LED points.*
Below: *A procedural animation of lifelike computer-generated plants—growing rapidly to fill Poison Ivy's lair—is then added to the scene.*

APPLICATION AND INTEGRATION

Ultimately, it all comes down to keeping three steps ahead of the current technology. Dykstra uses the example of the massive Gotham Observatory to demonstrate how computers can help to integrate the efforts of several key behind-the-scenes artists: "Because the dome was so large, and took a long time to build, in order to determine what kind of camera angles would work best, we built a three-dimensional mathematical model of the Observatory in the computer. A lot of the decisions were made in computer-generated models that could never have been done before by our production designer, director of photography and set construction people, and therefore preproduction becomes much more effective. We can be more decisive about things that we want to do. As a result, the money ends up on the screen rather than in changes after the fact.

"So the idea of using the computer in that capacity, based on its effort in the design phase, integrates into all facets of the work that we're doing, both visual effects and live action. And of course, the three-dimensional shots that we create in the computer can be edited together as animatics, which increases the collaborative effort. It's become a valuable tool, and it's surprised me how much we've come to rely on it in this short period of time.

"The speed with which the systems are developing is incredible," enthuses Dykstra, "and it provides us with an amazing tool for making images that are unlike any you've seen before. It gives us the flexibility to help production out when they run into a problem. Viewing audiences have become more sophisticated, so we are having to put more sophisticated images on film. Even though the cost of a given effect is coming down, the demand is for more complex effects.

"Filmmaking is a process of constant change. It seems that every week something new crops up, and it's turned all of the masters into students again, which is great. What it means is that when you set out to do a movie like *Batman & Robin*, you have to bite off more than you can chew. Because if you limit yourself to what you're capable of doing at the time the film is mounted, by the time the film is completed you'll be obsolete."

In the long run, Dykstra believes that "our challenge is to figure out how to apply these incredibly powerful new tools in a way that reflects style, talent and concept, as opposed to just shotgunning and grandstanding."

And is it wearying for him to constantly keep abreast of every new revolution in technology? "Are you kidding?" he asks with a smile spreading beneath his beard. "I love it. It keeps me alive. There's nothing better!"

And then, for John Dykstra, it's back to the drawing board...or as the case may be, the computer terminal, the soundstage, the miniatures facility or the inside of his ever-fertile mind.

PUTTING IT TOGETHER

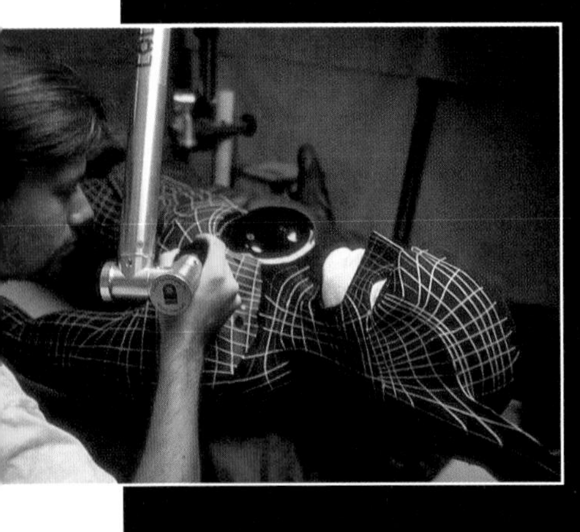

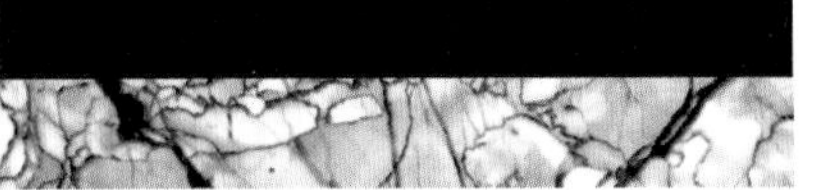

Contrary to the usual laws of reason, as far as making movies is concerned, it *isn't* over when it's over. Well after the last reel of film has wended its way through the camera, there are plenty of puzzle pieces that still need to be cemented together. *Batman & Robin* would have less than five months between the end of principal photography and its mid-June release date—perhaps a reasonable amount of time for a conventional film, but hardly enough for one with so many diverse elements needing to find their way into coherent form.

THE FILM EDITOR

Dennis Virkler is a man who would much rather be doing his job than talking about it. One of the industry's finest edi-

Right: *Batman's ultra-high-tech computer screens, both large and small.*
Below: *Robin (Chris O'Donnell), Batman (George Clooney) and Batgirl (Alicia Silverstone) set their minds to the tasks ahead.*

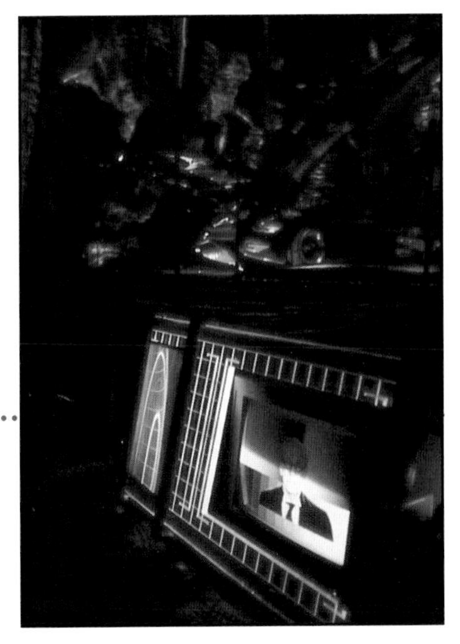

tors, Virkler received Academy Award nominations for his work on *The Hunt for Red October* and *The Fugitive*. *Batman & Robin* reunites Virkler with Joel Schumacher. "We have all been this way before," Virkler says. "We learned a lot from *Batman Forever*, which has made things easier on *Batman & Robin*. Also, Joel Schumacher has a great talent for casting—not just the actors, but his creative team as well. And his strength is that he trusts them to do their jobs well. This is also the fifth movie that I've done with Peter Macgregor-Scott, who is amazingly organized as well."

Virkler admits that the film is "absolutely the biggest challenge I've ever had. There are more than twice the number of visual effects shots than in *Batman Forever*, as well as large segments from the second unit." He reiterates what so many other *Batman & Robin* personnel have pointed out: that the interrelationships between the key creative staff are remarkable. "There's a lot of dialogue that doesn't have to be exchanged between us," says Virkler. "We begin to finish each other's sentences after a while. There's a synergy that takes place between all of us on this movie, and it allows us a way to get right to the core and get the job done.

"I'm also fortunate," continues Virkler, "in that I have a great team working with me in the editing room, including Mark Stevens as additional editor. We also have the capabilities now of cutting much faster than in the past because of the computerized Lightworks system. That really facilitates the speed and the ease of editing."

With Lightworks, an editor can instantaneously call up any frame or take of the movie at any time. "I'll tell you how much it helps," adds Virkler. "On *The Fugitive*, there were six of us who edited the movie, and if the Lightworks system had been up and running at that point, we could have done it with two. The consistency with which two editors can exchange material and present it to the director is phenomenal."

SOUND EDITORS

"Today's movie audiences expect a film to sound as good as it looks," says John Leveque, who with colleague Bruce Stambler handled the complex task of selecting, designing and editing the thousands of sound elements required for *Batman & Robin*.

Stambler adds, "A well-crafted soundtrack will help the audience to focus on a particular scene in a movie by complementing what's happening on the screen. What Joel Schumacher puts on the screen is the blueprint; we design the sound around the action, so that it reinforces the focus of a scene, yet without being distracting. There is a very fine line between too much and too little, so we carefully select the right combination of sound effects to get the perfect sound for each event in the film."

This talented pair of co-supervising

Right: *The magnificent expanse of the redesigned Batcave.*
Below: *George Clooney amply fits Batman's cowl.*
Bottom right: *The new Batmobile roars out of the Batcave, accompanied by Robin on his equally fleet Redbird motorcycle.*

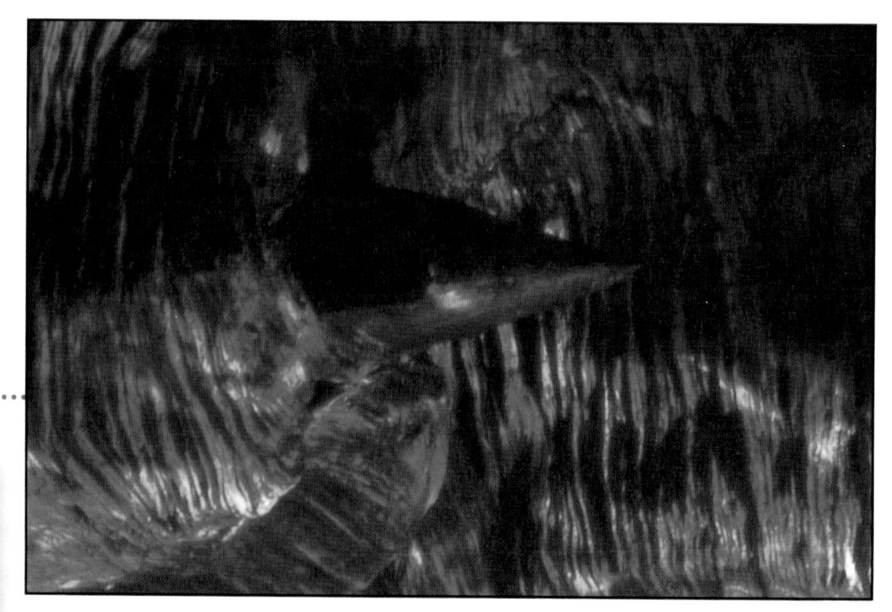

"The core of the Batmobile sound is an 800-horsepower, street-legal 1987 Buick Grand National with a wonderful turbocharger whine," notes Stambler. "All in all, we used 60 different, individual sounds to build the sound of the Batmobile."

One of Leveque's and Stambler's favorite sounds used in the film came about by accident. "We needed a large swooshing sound for Batman's cape," recalls Stambler. "We had already secured a number of recordings of bat wings that were very good, but we lacked a big sound that would really give the feeling of Batman rising into the air and moving off at high speed."

As fate would have it, the world-famous Warner Bros. Studios water tower had been covered in a massive tarpaulin. "During a windy rainstorm," Stambler continues, "the tarp came loose and ended up streaming off into the air held only by a single tether. We snuck under the tower with our microphone and a portable DAT recorder. What you hear in the movie includes the sound of this enormous tarp flapping, whipping and snapping around in the gale-force wind. It had exactly the right power, 'crack' and 'whoosh' that we needed!"

sound editors headed a team of experienced audio professionals from SoundStorm, the Burbank-based sound editorial house that has garnered five Academy Award nominations, including one for *Batman Forever*. Stambler won the 1996 Oscar for his work on *The Ghost and the Darkness*.

For many key scenes in *Batman & Robin*, Leveque and Stambler developed innovative sounds that would draw the audience into the high-intensity action. Leveque explains, "We wanted the Batmobile to sound exciting and bigger than life." To help create a part of the vehicle's multilayered sound, Leveque and Stambler visited the Rocket Dyne Space Shuttle facility in Canoga Park, California, where they recorded the intense blast of the Atlas rocket engine.

Right: *Batman (George Clooney) at the foot of the Wayne Manor grand staircase.*
Below: *Composer Elliot Goldenthal.*

THE COMPOSER

Just as Joel Schumacher redefined Batman in image, his choice of composer, Elliot Goldenthal, helped to re-create the character in music. One of the most highly respected, versatile and prolific of the newer generation of film music composers, Goldenthal won a Golden Globe Award and Oscar nomination for *Interview with the Vampire* and gained another Academy Award nomination in 1996 for *Michael Collins*.

In addition to *Batman Forever*, Goldenthal previously collaborated with Joel Schumacher on *A Time to Kill*, another powerful score that, typical of Goldenthal, avoided cliché at every turn (and brought the composer a Grammy nomination). The composer has impeccable "serious" music credentials, having also written symphonies and other orchestral pieces performed in international concert halls. He was even commissioned by the American Ballet Theatre to write a full-length ballet of *Othello*, which premiered one month before *Batman & Robin*.

On a visit in late January 1997 to Los Angeles from his New York base, Goldenthal's work on *Batman & Robin* was still ahead of him, but he was already excited by his latest collaboration with Schumacher. "At our best, Joel lets me go and be me," the composer says in his hotel suite. "However, he's a very commanding director, so if he doesn't like something, it's very difficult for me to talk him out of it. But as is often the case, that only serves to better the movie.

"Joel is musically astute. He was very brave with *A Time to Kill*. There was a lot of very unusual music in the film, and he supported that and mixed it brilliantly into the final sound design."

Coming into *Batman Forever*, Goldenthal was of course familiar with Danny Elfman's scores for Tim Burton's *Batman* and *Batman Returns*. "I saw the first two *Batman* movies, liked the music, but never referred to them again. I thought that Danny did fantastic work with Burton, but for *Batman Forever*, I needed to create a brand-new theme and a different approach.

"The thing that's been established about this new Batman world, which was created for the last film," Goldenthal continues, "is that the music is large and orchestral. And because Batman wears a black cape, lives in a cave and has a double life, you take it for granted that the music has a bit of darkness to it too. Then you also have the hero versus the villain, and you have a certain genre that's built in right there. Large, orchestral, dark, heroic, good versus evil.

"I've been seeing which themes from *Batman Forever* can carry over," adds Goldenthal, "because it's always nice to have a continuum if you can. It's obvious that Robin is a more major figure in this film, so I have to come up with a bigger and more heroic Robin theme. There also have to be new themes for Mr. Freeze and Poison Ivy. So I'm about to start developing these ideas into music."

As Goldenthal's work expands even more beyond the film world, where does he see himself going in the next few years? "I don't see any discrepancy at all between going back and forth from film to orchestral pieces or theatrical pieces," he states. "I've always taken film music very seriously, and have never looked down on it as an art form. I just like to achieve some balance between the different mediums—whether ballet, musicals, symphonies or films."

And the piano in the corner of his hotel suite is a reminder that wherever Elliot Goldenthal may be, the music goes right along with him.

THE FINAL SIGNAL

January 27, 1997.

There's nothing like the last day of a long, arduous shoot, even one that has by some miracle finished 10 days ahead of schedule. On set, the atmosphere is relaxed, but still precise and carefully directed. Joel Schumacher stages insert shots of Batgirl pulling on her "heroine suit" for the first time, Batman and Robin selecting their specialized gadgets from their respective vaults and, for extra punch, a few additional shots of Uma Thurman as Dr. Pamela Isley meeting her grisly fate in the tented Amazon laboratory. For this set-up, Thurman has to be covered with dirt, poisonous plants and live non-poisonous snakes ("I started the movie with snakes, and I'm ending it the same way," she laughs with a shudder after completing her final scene).

Simultaneously, there's a sense of increased activity and an almost palpable collective sigh of relief. We've done it. We've gotten through it. And maybe, we've *nailed* it.

Inside the production office annex, associate producer Mitch Dauterive and production coordinator Robin Mulcahy are overseeing their clerical staff, as files and computers are loaded into transfer boxes and hurried last-minute reports are written.

Outside the dome, transportation coordinator Craig Pinkard and his team of drivers are preparing to have the company trucks locked and loaded immediately after Schumacher calls the final "Cut!" and first assistant director Bill Elvin announces, in his most stentorian tones, "That's a wrap!" An almost plaintive blast from the *Queen Mary*'s foghorn sounds like a farewell to the *Batman & Robin* crew members who have labored in her shadow for five months.

Then, inside the darkened dome, when the crew returns from lunch, they're greeted by a remarkable, eerie sight: projected onto the huge curved interior wall of the building is the Bat-Signal.

This is a crew that has lived with Batman day in and out, understandably ho-humming after a few months at the common sight of the Caped Crusader and his crime-fighting partners walking to and from the set and maybe even catching a few winks during lunch break inside the Batcave, as if it were a Motel 6.

But this Bat-Signal is different. It isn't intended for a scene in the movie, it isn't designed for the visual effects department. It's just for the benefit of the company—special lighting designer John Tedesco's way of saluting his colleagues for months of hard work, and at the same time, saluting the legend that everyone involved with *Batman & Robin* has helped to renew and perpetuate.

For them—as for the millions of readers, television watchers and moviegoers who for 60 years have locked heart and soul into the timeless fable of the Caped Crusader, a good if sometimes troubled mortal who under cover of night endlessly battles the chaotic forces of evil for a common good—this special signal shines ever onward, projecting our shared past and hopeful future.

For them, Batman and Robin live...forever!

BATMAN™ & ROBIN™

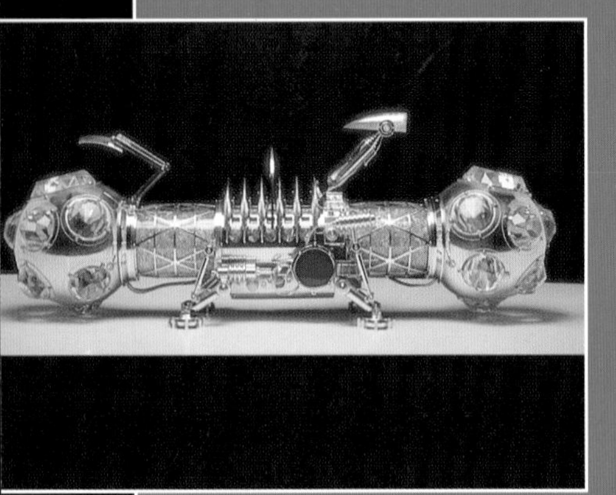

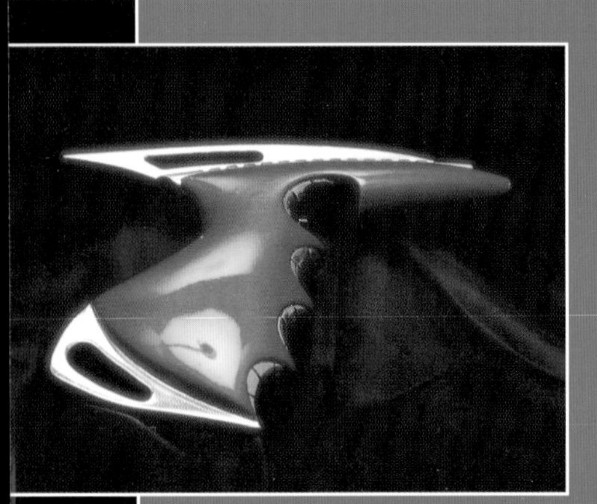

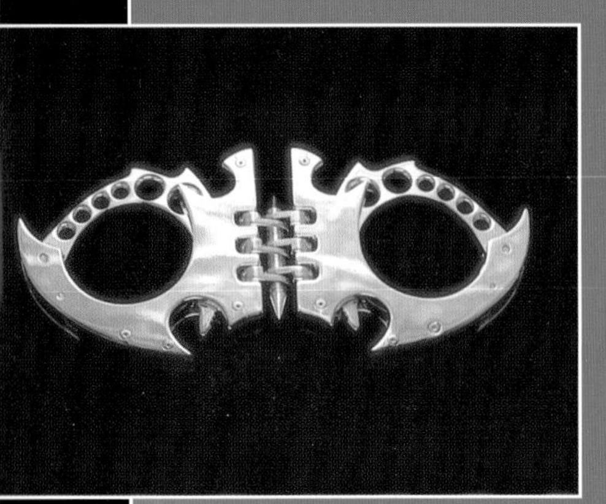

THE CAST

Mr. Freeze/Victor Fries	Arnold Schwarzenegger
Batman/Bruce Wayne	George Clooney
Robin/Dick Grayson	Chris O'Donnell
Poison Ivy/Dr. Pamela Isley	Uma Thurman
Batgirl/Barbara Wilson	Alicia Silverstone
Alfred Pennyworth	Michael Gough
Police Commissioner Gordon	Pat Hingle
Julie Madison	Elle Macpherson
Dr. Jason Woodrue	John Glover
Bane	Jeep Swenson
Nora Fries	Vendela Thommessen
Ms. B. Haven	Vivica A. Fox

THE FILMMAKERS

Music by	Elliot Goldenthal
Costume Designers	Ingrid Ferrin & Robert Turturice
Visual Effects by	John Dykstra
Film Editor	Dennis Virkler
Production Designer	Barbara Ling
Director of Photography	Stephen Goldblatt
Executive Producers	Benjamin Melniker & Michael E. Uslan
Based upon Batman characters created by	Bob Kane
And published by	DC Comics
Written by	Akiva Goldsman
Produced by	Peter Macgregor-Scott
Directed by	Joel Schumacher

Warner Bros. Pictures
A Time Warner Entertainment Company

The above credits are not all-inclusive and do not necessarily reflect final billing.